Palgrave Studies in Arab Cinema

Series Editors
Samirah Alkassim
Film and Video Studies
George Mason University
Fairfax, VA, USA

Nezar Andary
College of Humanities and Social Sciences
Zayed University
Abu Dhabi
United Arab Emirates

This series presents new perspectives and intimate analyses of Arab cinema. Providing distinct and unique scholarship, books in the series focus on well-known and new auteurs, historical and contemporary movements, specific films, and significant moments in Arab and North African film history and cultures. The use of multi-disciplinary and documentary methods creates an intimate contact with the diverse cultures and cinematic modes and genres of the Arab world. Primary documents and new interviews with directors and film professionals form a significant part of this series, which views filmmakers as intellectuals in their respective historical, geographic, and cultural contexts. Combining rigorous analysis with material documents and visual evidence, the authors address pertinent issues linking film texts to film studies and other disciplines. In tandem, this series will connect specific books to online access to films and digital material, providing future researchers and students with a hub to explore filmmakers, genres, and subjects in Arab cinema in greater depth, and provoking readers to see new frames of transnational cultures and cinemas.

Series Editors:

Samirah Alkassim is an experimental documentary filmmaker and Assistant Professor of Film Theory at George Mason University. She is the co-editor of the Palgrave Studies in Arab Cinema and her publications include the co-authored book The Cinema of Muhammad Malas (Palgrave, 2018), contributions to Cinema of the Arab World: Contemporary Directions in Theory and Practice (Palgrave, 2020), the Historical Dictionary of Middle Eastern Cinema, 2nd Edition (Rowman and Littlefield, 2020), as well as chapters in Refocus: The Films of Jocelyne Saab (Edinburgh University Press, 2021), Gaza on Screen (forthcoming 2022), and text book Global Horror: Hybridity and Alterity in Transnational Horror Film (Cognella Academic Publishing, forthcoming 2022) which she co-edited with Ziad El-Bayoumi Foty. She is currently writing a book, A Journey of Screens in 21st Century Arab Film and Media (Bloomsbury, forthcoming 2023) and editing a documentary about Jordanian artist Hani Hourani. She holds an MFA in Cinema from San Francisco State University and a BA in English Literature from Oberlin College.

Nezar Andary is Assistant Professor of Film and Literature at Zayed University in the College of Humanities and Sustainability Sciences. He has published literary translations, poetry, and articles on Arab documentary, and researched the relationship of Arab cinema to the recent Arab uprisings. Among his many involvements in Abu Dhabi, he directed a multilingual play for the Abu Dhabi Book Fair and organized an Environmental Documentary Film Series. In addition, he served as Artistic Director for Anasy Documentary Awards in 2010 and Artistic Director for the documentary series Perspectives and Retrospectives in 2013. He holds a PhD from the University of California, Los Angeles and was a Fulbright recipient conducting research in Syria.

Khadijeh Habashneh

Knights of Cinema

The Story of the Palestine Film Unit

Translated by
Samirah Alkassim and Nadine Fattaleh

Khadijeh Habashneh
Independent scholar
Amman, Jordan

Translated by
Samirah Alkassim
Film and Video Studies
George Mason University
Gaithersburg, MD, USA

Nadine Fattaleh
Media Culture and Communications
program of NYU
NYU
New York, NY, USA

ISSN 2731-4898   ISSN 2731-4901   (electronic)
Palgrave Studies in Arab Cinema
ISBN 978-3-031-18857-2   ISBN 978-3-031-18858-9   (eBook)
https://doi.org/10.1007/978-3-031-18858-9

This Palgrave Macmillan imprint is published by the registered company Springer Nature Switzerland AG.
The registered company address is: Gewerbestrasse 11, 6330 Cham, Switzerland

v

Fig. 1   Sulafa Jadallah, the first woman Arab cinematographer, at Al-Karameh, 1968

This book is dedicated to…
Sulafa Jadallah,
the first Knight and the first Arab woman cinematographer,
her fellow Knights of the Revolutionary Cinema,
Hani Jawharieh and Mustafa Abu Ali,
the heroic Martyrs and Cinematographers,
Ibrahim Nasser (Mutee') and Abdelhafeth Al-Asmar (Omar),
and all the Pioneers of the Palestinian Cinema.
Khadijeh Habashneh

FOREWORD

WHY THIS BOOK?

A book with a simple title, one that seems festive and provocative, arrives at a time when the provocative celebration is absent, *Knights of Cinema— Story of the Palestine Film Unit*, researched and written by Khadijeh Habashneh.

Its subject, however, pertains to an unquestionably serious matter defined by two objectives: a moral commitment to memorialize the struggle of young filmmakers from Palestine, Jordan, and other Arab countries, who gave their lives to their art and believed in its provocative—enlightening—message; and the preservation of cinematic memory. Some of these filmmakers were martyred, others were wounded and their lives disrupted, and a third group sacrificed their own dreams for a cause that went beyond individual considerations: the question of Palestine. This commitment participated in preserving a Palestinian cinematic memory that grew into a revolutionary context, faced multiple challenges, and lived long after 1982, *after* the Palestinian resistance left Beirut.

If, prior to leaving Beirut, the challenges of the birth of this cinema approached martyrdom, the loss of the archive after departure required an even more arduous effort to find and re-animate [or restore] it, even if it was incomplete.

This exhaustive effort, which took almost a decade, is what Khadijeh Habashneh, revealing great modesty, has called "writing and research." In rescuing the "documented memory," this text has preserved the struggle, suffering, and steadfastness of the Palestinians for more than two decades, depicting the misery of the camps, the fire of fedayeen operations and Israeli raids, and major tragic events such as the siege and fall of Tal Al-Za'atar in the summer of 1976.

With patience and persistent research, Habashneh has presented a cultural work of tremendous integrity and commitment. She has done this without seeking personal benefit, and without any institutional support.

Her book opens with two acknowledgments that are highly significant and demonstrate her conviction: First, "This year 2019 marks the 50th anniversary of the first Revolutionary Palestinian film to announce the image of the Palestinian people and their revolution to liberate their land." This acknowledgment turns the birth of the revolutionary cinema into the birth of the Palestinian revolution, linking a "new cinema" with a new struggle. This reveals the nature of Habashneh's book, with its unassuming title, as political-historical research, which reflects the transition of Palestinians from one state to another; it examines the uniqueness of the "revolutionary cinema," which is directed at a new audience, and distinct from the traditional cinema, whether Hollywood or Arab cinema. The second acknowledgment refers to the loyalty of the living to the dead, those who died for a just and universal human cause: "This year also marks the tenth anniversary of the absence of one of the founders of this cinema and the last of its knights, the Palestinian director Mustafa Abu Ali...." To counter the threat of oblivion, Habashneh chose to address the forgotten, and to recall and recount the bright era led and participated in by the late director.

This book was intended to recall a distinguished film fighter who lived and was devoted to his cause, sometimes facing rigid bureaucratic attitudes and cultural disbelief that a film could be a combative tool adopted by all the revolutionary movements in the world. His suffering was intensified by the difficulty of beginnings, because unlike the non-refugee revolutionary movements that developed their cinematic art after their victories, Mustafa Abu Ali started from a Palestinian condition where "there was no cinema and no stability." He was obsessed with the idea of establishing and securing the materials and technical effort *necessary to build 'what does not exist'* which was a commonly held idea among Palestinian revolutionaries at that time.

Perhaps the obstinate connection between the beginning of the armed revolution and the beginning of the revolutionary film is what made Mustafa summon all his strength and mentor a generation of young people who learned the principles of cinema work while practicing it. For this he assembled Arab and Palestinian efforts, which culminated in meeting committed artists from all over the world. Although it was and still is abbreviated in the simple term "documentary film," the efforts of Mustafa Abu Ali and his companions were epic: the photographers were fighters first, and their relationship with photography was very limited until they were trained; their cameras were surrounded by dust and bullets. They often fell on the battlefield, like the martyr Hani Jawhariyyeh,[1] who left a secure job and chose to film mountain battles very far from safety.

While Habashneh states in the subtitle of her book, "The first film unit to accompany a national liberation movement from the beginning," the real subject of her book is the rendering of the lives of Palestinian film pioneers in their revolutionary dreams and sacrifices. As a veteran revolutionary, she recorded what she had experienced with the pioneers of the Palestine Film Unit, adding to that many testimonies, whether mentioned in a silent written form, or the oral accounts of people who are still alive. She wanted to restore the Palestinian cinematic truth, after it had been forgotten.

Habashneh traced the effects of a subject she had lived and experienced and went from the status of the witness artist to the historian, who sees, inquires, examines, and travels to build a cinematic document worthy of cinematic fighters. Through her efforts she has archived and restored what was once archived and lost. She searched for it in more than one human reference and city, and it is coincidental that the film archive she and her husband had kept in a safe place in Beirut ended up in the Israeli intelligence records, hence the importance of what the knights of Palestinian cinema had accomplished.

Habashneh has made a long effort to preserve the Palestinian film archive, to resurrect it and bring it back to life. In this she is expressing her loyalty to its creators and recognizing its national importance, as the archive classifies the following: humanitarian documents, the people of the camps, the efforts of the cinema pioneers, documents about many battles not least the Battle of Al-Karameh, and artistic documents that witnessed the difficulties of the making of the Palestinian revolutionary cinema.

As an author, she has taken memory as her solid reference, recognizing that those with no memory are without history, and that memory is a living existence that needs to be activated, cared for, and structured. Her

---

[1] Although the spelling of "Jawhariyyeh" as is done here is common, the rest of this book observes the spelling used by the family of Hani Jawharieh.

long quest to recover the films is an example of memory activation, and her book aims to celebrate what should not be forgotten. In both cases, she has recounted a series of experiences including her own, parts from Mustafa Abu Ali's life history and his cinematic visions, film manifestos and festivals, and the experiences of anonymous peers who fought through their militant films. She has mentioned their names, highlighted their lives, and illuminated their stories and sad tales.

Through the content of this book, Habashneh has sought authenticity by using unembellished language. She has prioritized a clear and factual writing style which does justice to the fedayeen in the field of cinema, rather than concerning herself with verbal sophistication. This gives a lesson about the loyalty of the living to the dead. It keeps its sincerity in spite of all the frequent battles of the Palestinians and explores the credibility of the artist.

Finally, this book is a testament to the urgency of memory for identity, history, and, in the case of the Palestinian struggle, morality. It is worth reading.

August 30, 2019
Amman, Jordan

Faisal Darraj

Faisal Darraj is an award-winning author, philosopher, and literary critic based in Amman, Jordan, born in Palestine. His contributions to contemporary literary and cultural discourse in the Arab world are formidable, including his book *Theory of the Novel and the Arabic Novel*, and translations of European and French philosophy into Arabic.

ACKNOWLEDGMENTS

At the end of extensive work on this English edition of the book *Knights of Cinema*, I would like first to thank the researcher, film critic, and historian Pablo Robledo (a cross-country skier), who generously gave me the right to use important quotations from his book *Montoneros y Palestina*.

I am deeply grateful to Dr. Faisal Darraj for his precious time and sincerity in writing the foreword to this book. I am also deeply appreciative of Samirah Alkassim for her attentive reading of the English translation, and for her devoted effort and close engagement as an editor of this entire manuscript.

I would also like to acknowledge the following friends and colleagues: professor of photography Samir Faraj, novelist Rashad Abu Shawar, film critic Qais Al Zubaidi, researcher and author Nazih Abu Nidal, and journalist and photographer Ramzi Rasi, for their testimonies on the pioneering role of the Palestine Film Unit in the revolutionary cinema.

I am immensely grateful to all my colleagues for their precious time, information, and memories, and for granting the right to use them in my book: Janette Fattaleh, Amneh Naser, Elias Sanbar, Salah Abu Hannoud, Mahmoud Majd, Adil Al-Kesbeh, Tawfeq Musa Khalil, Mahmoud Nofal, Khalil Sa'adeh, and Yousef Al Shayeb. I also thank my colleagues, Omar Al-Rashidi and Shaher Al-Soumi, for the revision of some details from their experience, and to colleague Yousef Qutob who shared many pictures from the photography archive of the PFU/PCI.

Finally, I could not have written this without the help from family members of the pioneers of the revolutionary cinema, and those of the writers and journalists who documented this movement. For granting their permission to use quotations from their interviews or their relatives' writings and interviews, I thank the following: Abdelraheem Jadallah, Sulafa's brother; Husam Riyad Jawharieh, Hani's nephew; Dama'a, Rasmi, and Fatmeh Abu Ali, Mustafa's siblings; Majida Al-Hourani, Tayseer Al-Najjar's widow; and Sahar and Shahira Abu Ghanimeh, sister and daughter of Hassan Abu Ghanimeh.

CONTENTS

ABOUT THE AUTHOR

Khadijeh Habashneh, also known as Khadijeh Abu Ali, is a researcher, filmmaker, and political and women's rights activist. She holds a master's degree in psychology and began her career as a clinical psychologist in a psychiatric clinic in Jordan, where she worked from 1968 until 1971. One of the founding members of the core of the General Union of Palestinian Women, which was one of the most active bodies of the PLO during the 1970s, Khadijeh was also a founding member of the Palestinian Cinema Institution (PCI) which formed in 1974 and was responsible for creating and maintaining the PCI's archive and the cinematheque from 1974 to 1982. Her film *Children Without Childhood* (1979) was recently restored, but the other film, *Women of My Country,* disappeared during the IDF siege of Beirut in 1982.She has represented Palestinian women and the Palestinian cause at numerous regional and international conferences and forums from 1975 until 2005 and is a founding member of several social and cultural organizations and institutes working on women's issues and human rights, such as the Center for Women Studies in Jordan for which she served as Vice President from 1989 to 1992. She has coordinated national campaigns for enhancing women's participation in elections in Jordan (1996) and Palestine (2002–2005) and is a board member of the UNESCO-designated Palestinian Women's Research and Documentation

Center (PWRDC), which is dedicated to developing documentation and research on the condition and status of Palestinian women and girls and gender issues.

Khadijeh has also served as a lecturer in psychology and gender issues at Al-Quds University in Jerusalem from 2002 to 2004 and has published several studies on women's issues, in addition to literary writings and articles.

LIST OF FIGURES

Introduction

This book narrates the story of a group of exceptional and pioneering filmmakers. It is a story of the first cinema unit to work hand in hand with the armed Palestinian national liberation movement since its inception.

I find myself writing this story with multiple and diverse narrative voices, perhaps because of my aversion to the traditional documentary style of writing. It is perhaps also that I am close to the founders, and I demand accuracy and integrity in documenting a large part of the journey of the Palestine Film Unit (PFU) after five decades have passed since its inception, by making use of the oral history method. A large portion of this book is narrated through the voices of members of the unit who are still alive, or their close friends and relatives who lived the early days of the PFU and its development. I have also relied on segments of what members of the PFU have written or said in interviews, and some writings by their contemporaries, in addition to my personal experiences. The research and interviews for this book extended over many years, between June 2014 and July 2019, because of my inability to dedicate myself full time to the work, and because my interlocutors are located in different countries.

In the second half of the 1960s, three of the earliest graduates of the cinema institutes in Cairo and London met and decided to join the fedayee movement, or the Palestinian National Movement (Fatah), after its inception following the defeat of the Arab armies in the June 5, 1967, war. They established a film unit in 1968, which produced its first film in 1969.

This book was originally published in Arabic in 2019, for the fiftieth anniversary of the first Palestinian revolutionary film. The English translation is true to the original with some additional information and clarifications here and there, in the hopes of reaching a wider audience about an extraordinary film movement that announced to the world the image of the Palestinian people and their struggle to liberate their homeland from Zionist occupation. This image had been rendered invisible in international news through the Zionist hegemony over capital and global media networks. The year 2019 also marked the tenth anniversary of the passing of one of the founders and knights of the Palestine Film Unit, the director Mustafa Abu Ali, who died on July 30, 2009.

The PFU launched Palestinian cinema through the participation of a number of progressive filmmakers from Palestine, the Arab states, and the world. It shaped a global militant cinema movement around the Palestinian cause. I return to document the journey of the PFU after its history has been neglected and its leading role has been marginalized. I also write in response to inaccuracies and false pretenses put forward by narcissistic filmmakers or journalists and critics who advance a stereotypical understanding of the particular context of the PFU.

This revolutionary cinema unit, and its founders, the artists, and courageous knights of cinema, must be celebrated for its martyrs on the battlefield, and its filmmakers who have sacrificed many of their personal dreams in service of the cause of their people under occupation and in exile. The PFU members innovated a unique militant cinematic language and created an international phenomenon out of the Palestinian cause in the 1970s. They deserve on this occasion to be remembered and celebrated in recognition of their leadership and sacrifice, and for safeguarding the memory of their experiences for the coming generations.

Khadijeh Habashneh

CHAPTER 1

Origins in Amman: Scenes and Narratives

The scene below is one I have long imagined, based on what I have been told, about the first meetings between Sulafa Jadallah, Hani Jawharieh, and Mustafa Abu Ali in Jordan in the late 1960s. While most of this book is based on testimonies and published accounts, it seems fitting to begin as if we are in a film about the origins of a film movement, establishing the characters of the three knights who began it, and dedicated their lives to it, yet who are no longer with us.

Place: Office of Ali Siyam,[1] manager of the Cinema Department of the Jordanian Ministry of Information.

Date: One day in September, 1966.

Time: Around 11:00 in the morning.

The manager, Mr. Ali, leaves the room with the young Hani Jawharieh, recently returned from London after completing a scholarship program sponsored by the British Council in Amman through the Ministry of Information.

Mr. Ali leads the way saying, "I have a surprise for you. I want to introduce you to the cinematographer Sulafa Jadallah. My friend, Sulafa is the

---

[1] Ali Isma'il Siyam was the manager of the Cinema Department at the Jordanian Ministry of Information from 1964 to 1970. He directed the Jordanian newsreels that preceded theatrical film screenings and produced many documentary films including *Exodus*, *The Scorched Earth*, and *Zahrat Al-Mada'in*.

© The Author(s), under exclusive license to Springer Nature Switzerland AG 2023
K. Habashneh, *Knights of Cinema*, Palgrave Studies in Arab Cinema, https://doi.org/10.1007/978-3-031-18858-9_1

first cinematographer not just here, in Jordan, but in the Arab world. And there's a story she will tell you about her studies at the Higher Institute of Cinema in Cairo."

Before they arrive, Sulafa enters accompanied by the photography crew with their equipment.

Mr. Ali approaches "How are things, Sulafa? You've just come back from filming? I have a surprise for you."

Sulafa: "Hopefully it's good news. How are you?"

Everyone enters the cinematography room. The crew returns the film equipment to its place, then they leave.

Sulafa sits down and invites Mr. Ali and Hani to join her: "Come in please. Mr. Ali, what is the surprise?"

He replies: "I'd like to introduce you, Sulafa, to our new cinematographer, Hani Jawharieh. He recently returned from London, where he was sent on a scholarship by our ministry to study cinematography. When you were first appointed here, you may have heard us speak about a student who would soon graduate. This is him!"

Sulafa welcomes Hani and expresses her pleasure over his return, "Alhamdullah 'Al-Salameh, and welcome! It's great that there are two of us now! This will make the work easier and more pleasant."

Mr. Ali rises to leave the room as he says, "Yella [Ok], I will leave you to get to know each other. Sulafa, tell him about the nature of our work."

As soon as he leaves, Hani approaches Sulafa with a question, "First, I am surprised to actually find a female cinematographer in our country. Mr. Ali told me there is a story behind your education. Will you tell me, Miss Sulafa?"

Sulafa replies, "Ya Sidi, I've loved photography since my childhood. My brother was a fine artist working in a studio in Nablus. I loved looking at the photos he took, and asked him to teach me how to use the camera. Then, we started shooting together and we captured many scenes of life and people in Nablus. When I finished secondary school, I wanted to study photography, and I started asking around about where I could go. I discovered that an institute for cinema recently opened in Egypt, and I decided to study there. My parents didn't object, but it wasn't easy for them to be comfortable with me studying alone in Egypt.

My mother accompanied me and stayed until the female dormitory opened. But the story hasn't even yet begun. When I went to the institute, they refused to enroll me in the cinematography department because they thought it was difficult for women. I insisted and made several phone calls to get an appointment with the director of the institute, Mr. Mohammad Karim.[2] At our first meeting, he initially refused to allow me to register. Then when he saw that I was adamant, he agreed to let me in at my own risk. Finally! I registered, thank God, and succeeded in proving myself and my skills."

THE FIRST KNIGHT, SULAFA JADALLAH

Sulafa was born in Nablus on May 21, 1941, to a conservative family who were nonetheless open to life and new ideas.

Abdelraheem Jadallah[3] Recalls Sister Sulafa's Youth

"Sulafa enjoyed photography very early in her life, and what helped was my older brother Rima's[4] photography studio, which was full of cameras she would use to take photos. At first, she used simple cameras but as my brother noticed her enthusiasm, he allowed her to use more sophisticated ones with special features. Sulafa learned to develop and print her own film, which increased her enthusiasm and self-confidence. He encouraged her to develop her skills and asked her to photograph veiled women in the studio, allowing her to experiment creatively.

"Sulafa was culturally active. She loved reading and writing and excelled in her studies especially in Arabic language. She was involved in public speaking and school plays, as well as girl-scouts and sports activities.

"As her work with Rima' developed, they established an association for people who, like them, enjoyed photography and painting. It was like an arts association that many people joined, including the late Yahya Habash,[5]

---

[2] Mohammad Karim, writer, producer, and director, is one of the first film directors in Egypt, known for his musical films. He was the first director of the Higher Institute of Cinema in 1959.

[3] Abdelraheem Jadallah, Sulafa's younger brother, lives in Syria. This memory was presented in a letter obtained at the request of the author on February 27, 2018, who was unable to meet Abdelraheem personally due to the ongoing war in Syria.

[4] Rima' Jadallah, Sulafa's eldest brother, began his career as a fine artist and then shifted toward photography. He and Sulafa established the Society of Art Enthusiasts in Nablus in the 1950s.

[5] Yahya Habash, geological engineer, joined Fatah in its early days and was later known as Sakher Habash (Abu Nizar). He became one of its most prominent political leaders in addition to being a writer and fine artist.

and they collaborated later with the Palestinian artist Ismail Shammout,[6] who graduated from the Fine Arts College in Cairo. Together, they organized several art exhibitions in Nablus, Jenin, Toulkarem and Ramallah in the 1950s.

"Sulafa graduated from Al-'Aishiyeh High School and obtained the Matric certificate in 1959–1960.[7]

"Her interest in photography, in addition to the encouragement from Rima' and my mother, led her to study in the cinematography department of the Higher Institute of Cinema in Cairo. She travelled to Cairo with my mother, may her soul rest in peace, to register at the institute. At first, Sulafa's request to enroll in the cinematography department was met with resistance by the registration committee, on the pretext that the work would be very hard for her as a woman. As she and my mother continued to insist, their efforts were aided by the famous Egyptian actor Abdel-Wareth 'Asar, who was a professor there, and his brother the actor and photographer Hussein 'Asar, who was the administrative director.

"They both helped Sulafa meet with the institute's executive director who at the time was the famous film director Mohammad Karim. At first, he said that it would be difficult for Sulafa, as there were no female cinematographers, not even in America or Europe, and he suggested she choose another department. But with her continued insistence, he finally accepted her into the cinematography department in 1960–1961.

"Sulafa proved herself and was respected and admired by her teachers and fellow students alike. She accompanied her colleagues wherever they went, no matter the challenges she faced.

"Among her closest friends and collaborators were the important cinematographer Samir Faraj[8] and the actor Hasan Youssef.[9] The three always collaborated on projects including, of course, their graduation

---

[6] Ismail Shammout was among the first Palestinian artists. He graduated in the late 1950s from the Fine Arts College in Cairo and later studied art in Rome.

[7] The Matric Certificate was awarded upon completion of high school until 1959/1960. In 1961/1962 it changed to the Tawjihi Certificate of secondary school.

[8] Samir Faraj, prominent cinematographer in Egypt, later became a professor at the Higher Institute of Cinema in Cairo. He later directed the cinematography department at the Media Production City.

[9] Hasan Youssef, a well-known Egyptian actor, became famous in the 1960s for playing teenage roles.

project. They can speak of her with more detail than I, in this respect. Throughout all her years of study, she continuously received high grades, and graduated from the institute with distinction in 1963–1964. She also participated in filming with the esteemed professor Waheed Farid,[10] although I do not remember which films exactly."

Memory of Samir Faraj,[11] Sulafa's colleague from the Higher Institute of Cinema

"Alllahhhhh … God … You've reminded me of the most beautiful person I've ever met. Sulafa, may her soul rest in peace, was the icon of our group for her enthusiasm and liveliness at work, her manners and taste. She was an angel.

"She was quiet and kind, but very hard working. Being the only woman among nine men, the professors held her as the benchmark for assessing us. They would always say, 'Look at Sulafa, look at what she has done, she is better than all of you.' No doubt, she excelled in her studies, both in the theoretical understanding and in the practical work. I just received a photo of our class group taken a few days before graduation, and she's standing in the middle. I will send it to you." (Fig. 1.1)

Abdelraheem Jadallah Continues Narrating Sulafa's Story

"Sulafa graduated from the institute in 1964 and returned to Nablus. She took on numerous projects with my brother Rima' in his studio, which was named after him. One of the most important projects was photographing the city of Nablus and its villages, transferred to 8mm film. They also covered parties, sports festivals, and advertisements. When the Ministry of Information in Amman announced that it was recruiting photographers and filmmakers, Sulafa applied and was appointed as a cinematographer at the end of 1965 or the beginning of 1966."

---

[10] Egyptian cinematographer Waheed Farid (1919–1998), known as the "Sheikh" of cinematographers, was among the first to study color film in England.

[11] The testimony of the photographer Samir Faraj was obtained on May 20, 2018, in an interview conducted by the author in Cairo, where Faraj lives.

Fig. 1.1 Sulafa Jadallah among her colleagues at the Higher Institute of Cinema in Cairo, including Samir Faraj sitting in the middle

HANI JAWHARIEH

Born on October 26, 1939, Hani was raised in a household nourished by the arts and a rich cultural heritage. His uncle was the well-known musician and historian Wasif Jawhariyyeh.[12]

Recollections from Hani's Brother, Riyad Jawharieh[13]

"After the exodus in 1948, Hani's family moved temporarily to Jericho, waiting for the situation to settle down. When the Palestinians were formally registered at the beginning of 1950, my father worked for the

---

[12] This is how Wasif Jawhariyyeh is correctly spelled in Salim Tamari and Issam Nassar's book *The Storyteller of Jerusalem: The Life and Times of Wasif Jawhariyyeh (1904–1948)*.

[13] Riyad Jawharieh is the youngest and only brother of the martyred artist Hani Jawharieh. He was born in Jerusalem and studied calligraphy and design at the Fine Arts College in Cairo. He worked with the Fatah Movement, with the Occupied Territories department. His recollections were taken in an interview conducted by the author on October 16, 2016.

Fig. 1.2 Sulafa and Hani prepare for filming during their work at the Jordanian Ministry of Information, 1967

United Nations Relief and Works Agency (UNRWA), and our family was not counted as refugees.

"Hani developed his interest in photography in secondary school. At first, he had a camera with a hand crank. Afterwards, he used a camera with a black box, until he received a small, advanced camera capable of taking good photographs upon his visit to the Damascus International Exhibition with my father."

Riyad said that he remembers that his older brother Hani always asked him to buy a photography journal from the magazine and newspaper merchant Abed Da'ana. Abed used to display his magazines and newspapers on strings atop the wall of the Dar Hindiyeh building, a famous building in Al-Musrara, a neighborhood in Jerusalem.

He also recalls Hani involving him in photography experiments. For example, Hani would photograph him in front of a reflective surface like a slide on a wall, asking him to look attentively at the surface as if he were staring at the Eiffel Tower. He also used to experiment with effects like creating fog by using women's nylon socks on the camera lens (Fig. 1.2).

Hani completed his secondary studies at the Bishop School in Jerusalem in 1957 and worked for a short while at his cousin's eyewear store. After that, he worked at the Women's Teachers College in Al-Tireh, Ramallah, as the head of the audiovisual department. He left that job in 1962–1963 to study cinematography at the Higher Institute of Cinema in Cairo.

In 1964, Hani's father, Mr. Fakhri Jawharieh, heard of scholarships announced by the Jordanian Ministry of Information to support cinema studies in London. When Hani learned of the opportunity, he left his studies at the Higher Institute of Cinema and headed to Amman to apply for the scholarship. This is how he went to study cinematography in London in 1964, graduated in mid-1966, and returned to join the Department of Cinema in the Ministry of Information, where he met Sulafa Jadallah who was working there as a cinematographer.

Hani and Sulafa often discussed the nature of their training at the institutes from which they graduated, and they shared their early enthusiasm for photography. They developed a friendship and professional comradery through their work that intensified after the June 1967 war. This was forged in their joint efforts to photograph the suffering of the uprooting of hundreds of thousands of Palestinian refugees who crossed the wooden bridge over the Jordan River after the Israeli army's occupation of what remained of Palestine in the West Bank. They photographed the displacement of refugees to schoolyards and mosques, and then their relocation to refugee camps around Jordan. They also photographed the tragedy of those injured by the napalm phosphoric weapons, whether they were soldiers involved in the battle or civilians who were hurt while fleeing.

Riyad recalls Hani describing how he was sent by the Ministry of Information to photograph with the Jordanian army in Nablus during the 1967 war, although Hani did not mention any details about the nature of his participation or about the army's retreat.

As the effects of the war slowly dissipated in the second half of 1967, the young Mustafa Abu Ali completed his degree in directing at the London School of Film Technique, which became known as the London Film School in 1969.

Hani and Mustafa Abu Ali Meet at the Cinema Department of the Ministry of Information

The recent young graduate, Mustafa Abu Ali, enters the building of the Ministry of Information in Jabal Amman, and asks the first person he encounters at the entrance:

"Excuse me, where can I find the office of the general manager of the Cinema Department?"

Someone replies, "Take a right, continue straight ahead to the last office."

Mustafa heads toward the manager's office and knocks on the door until he is invited to come in. He enters the office and is surprised to find Hani Jawharieh who gets up enthusiastically to greet him.

"Welcome Mustafa, Abu Staif![14] You're finally here. Alhamdullah 'al Salameh. Welcome!"

The manager, Mr. Ali Siyam, rises: "Welcome. Hani has spoken about you so much it's given me a headache."

Mustafa responds: "Thank you, thank you, Mr. Ali."

Hani interrupts, "We have been waiting for you, as the new director, to complete the team. Welcome. I have missed you. Mr. Ali let's inform Sulafa. Actually, let's go surprise her. I've already told her so much about you, Mustafa."

Hani gets up, Mustafa follows, but Mr. Ali excuses himself, "You guys go ahead, I have to meet his excellency, the minister."

Mustafa Abu Ali

Mustafa Abu Ali was born in the village of Al-Malha, in the district of Jerusalem on November 25, 1940. He studied in Jerusalem until the second grade, when his family was forced to flee to Bethlehem in 1948 after news of the Deir Yassin massacre. There, he completed elementary school. He would spend the rest of his life recalling the daffodils in the orchard of his home in Al-Malha. He also recalled his attachment to the music lessons that were taught in elementary school in both Jerusalem and Bethlehem, and the way he used to run away to listen to the organ playing at the Church of Nativity in Bethlehem during religious celebrations.

Mustafa Describes Al-Malha[15]

"I still remember our house exactly as it is, and my grandfather's house in the heart of the village. I remember the name of the school where I studied for only two years before the occupation. I remember the mosque, the

---

[14] This is a common nickname for Mustafa.

[15] Interview by the journalist Yousef Al-Shayeb, conducted just a few days before Mustafa's death, and published in *Al-Ayyam* newspaper on August 4, 2009.

vineyards and the olive groves. I remember them very well. I visited Al-Malha in 1999. I had to sneak in. I tried to visit our house, but it was demolished.

"My relationship to cinema began there as different groups, I don't remember exactly who, screened various films, some for children, projected on a wall in the village. This was an indescribable pleasure!"

More Memories of Cinema[16]

"During my childhood, cinema was something I just couldn't get enough of, like sweets. At that time, my relationship to it was as an enchanted viewer. The first film I ever saw a film was in 1947 when I was 7 years old. It was about planting tomatoes and was screened in the square of the village (Al-Malha) on the wall of one of the houses. As a result of the forced displacement in Palestine in 1948, I fled with my family to Bethlehem where there was a cinema hall that regularly showed films. My older brother and I always had one aim, to get money from our parents for a movie ticket, but this was not always possible. Because of our strong urge to watch films, we resorted to different sneaky tricks. Most times, we were successful in watching the second half of the film."

Memories from Mustafa's Siblings[17]

Mustafa's eldest sister, **Dama'a Abu Ali**, recalls "how mischievous he was," as he used to jump on the sheets and blankets while she was folding them, and scribble and draw on the sheets forcing her to rewash them. Despite how this behavior delayed her housework, she tolerated it because "he was usually a calm, caring and good-hearted kid." She adds:

> When we moved to Bethlehem, Mustafa did not like attending the UNRWA school because it was set up in a tent and was not as organized as his old school in Jerusalem. He wanted to enroll in the national government school,

---

[16] These memories of Mustafa were written during an interview by journalist Tayseer Al-Najjar. The script of the interview was found among Mustafa's papers without reference to the date or publication details. The context of the conversation reveals it was conducted in the late 1990s; it became known later that Al-Najjar used to write for the Jordanian newspaper *Al Arab Al Yawm (The Arab Today)*.

[17] The memories of Mustafa's siblings were obtained during a social visit with the family requested by the author on July 30, 2018.

and started to scheme with his eldest brother, who knew that our mother hid money beneath the mattresses. They both took their certificates and my mother's money and went to the national school where they would not have been allowed to register because refugees could only attend UNRWA schools. However, when the headmaster saw that they were both students at the top of their class, he allowed them to register.

Mustafa's sister **Fatima**, who was a few years younger, recalls:

What I remember most about Mustafa when he was young, is how he used to make his own toys out of wires and old bottle caps. He made cars, trucks, buses and people, which he loved sharing with his friend. When we were preparing to leave from Kurzah (the village we had initially fled to from Al-Malha) to Bethlehem, he refused to ride the truck unless he could bring all his toys with him, and he had very many. My mother was forced to beg the truck driver to carry all of them. He also used to perform his own films in front of us. He would mount my mother's white headscarf on the wall and animate his handmade toys in front of a light to produce moving shadows. We really enjoyed this.

In 1952, Mustafa's family moved to Amman, where there were more work opportunities for his father who was a stone mason. Mustafa resumed his studies at Al-Husain College and was among the high-achieving students in the Matric exam at the end of high school. He received a scholarship for a year-long program in public health at the American University of Beirut. Upon graduating, he worked as an employee in the public health department of the Jordanian Ministry of Health for almost a year and a half. He then received a job offer at an American facility in the Saudi Arabian city Al-Khubar, and from there, he got a scholarship to study in America.

It was at this point that I first met Mustafa and his family—just before he traveled to Saudi Arabia—because I was friends with his sister Fatimah, whom I regularly spent time with. He was the handsome young man who I sometimes overheard trying to play the violin. A friendship and relationship of mutual interest grew between us because of our shared interest in the arts. He was interested in reading and music, while I was interested in reading and theatre. We started exchanging books and classical music records. At that time, I was in my third year of preparatory school, just before secondary school.

In mid-1964, Mustafa returned as an architecture student enrolled at the University of California, Berkeley. After completing almost three years of studies he discovered that architecture was not for him, even though he was three semesters away from graduating. He initially came to Cairo as I was completing my first year of university studies there. He was searching for an opportunity to study music after realizing that it was his true calling. He also wanted to be close to me, as we had developed a relationship of mutual affection since we first met in Amman before his travel to America, and we continued to be in touch every now and then. But where is a twenty-four-year-old man to find an opportunity to study music, when people usually start at a younger age?

Shortly after his return, and during a family visit to Amman, the Jordanian Ministry of Information announced the availability of scholarships to study cinema in London, offered through the British Council. This announcement was a golden opportunity for Mustafa, so he applied to one of those scholarships. Rasmi Abu Ali,[18] his older brother recalls, "Mustafa received the scholarship after shocking the head of the council because he scored the highest among all applicants."

At the cinema institute, Mustafa got to know Hani Jawharieh, who received a scholarship to study cinematography. They became close friends, as they both felt, with time, that they completed and complemented one another. Hani was the cinematographer with a delicate and sensitive eye. Mustafa was the young man who loved art and aspired to express his dreams and worries as a Palestinian, displaced from his homeland.

In the second half of 1967, Mustafa completed his studies at the London School of Film Technique and returned to Jordan to work at the cinema department of the Ministry of Information. He directed the film *Palestinian Right* in 1968, filmed by Hani and Sulafa. Around this time, Mustafa and his colleagues Sulafa and Hani joined the Fatah Information Office and established the department of photography.

I came to know Hani through Mustafa's letters when he began studying in London. I learned of Hani's return to Jordan through my participation in the meetings of the newly established Jordanian theatre troupe, which were held on the second floor of the Ministry. I would stop to meet

---

[18] Rasmi Abu Ali, Mustafa's brother, was a well-known writer and journalist. He was one of the important broadcasters of "Sawt Falastin" (Voice of Palestine) in Cairo since 1964, which was the official broadcaster of the Palestine Liberation Organization (PLO). He also published numerous short stories, poems, and one novella. His recollection was obtained through a casual social meeting requested by the author, July 30, 2018.

and greet Hani and would also ask about Mustafa who had stopped sending letters. After that, I met Sulafa and Hani upon Mustafa's graduation and his work in the cinema department. It was also the time I reconnected with Mustafa, and we decided to get engaged in mid-1968. At that point, I had already begun my job as a clinical psychologist, besides being a member in the Jordanian theater troupe.

One day, as we were preparing for our engagement, I told Mustafa that I had sent an application to join the fedayeen[19] just after the June war and its catastrophic results. They hadn't contacted me yet, but explained that when they do, the work with them would be secret. Mustafa smiled and said:

> What a relief. I was not sure how to tell you that I joined the revolution after Sulafa recommended and recruited me. I can ask her to inquire about your request and to introduce you. She is close with the revolution leadership.

Hani and Mustafa joined the Fatah movement through Sulafa's relationship to its leadership. This relationship had developed through Sulafa's previous participation with the organization supporting the Families of Martyrs and Prisoners Society, and her engagement with photographing the fedayeen and their martyrs which she used to capture with her personal camera and print them at home using her own equipment.

This is how I initially joined the Fatah movement, composed of the fedayeen with whom I wanted to work. This was, in my opinion, the most important work that could be done at the time.

Hind Jawharieh,[20] Hani's Wife, Recalls Their Early Days

"I used to know Hani as he was known to everyone, as a man from a well-known artistic family. After the war of 1967, I joined the Fatah movement, and met him when he worked at the Jordanian Ministry of Information with Sulafa Jadallah. They organized with Fatah, and Sulafa was the one who recruited Hani in 1967. There weren't many offices for the

---

[19] The word "fedayeen" means "freedom fighters" and, until mid-1969, referred specifically to Al-'Asifah military force and the Fatah movement in particular, or the Palestinian Revolution in general.

[20] Hind Jawharieh (real name: Janette Fattaleh), a Jerusalemite woman who joined the Fatah movement in its early days, was obliged to leave for Jordan when her connection to Fatah was revealed. She married Hani Jawharieh in 1970. Her memories were shared in an interview conducted by the author on October 25, 2017.

revolution in Amman, but Hani, Sulafa and Mustafa established a photography department housed in a joint office with the Families of the Martyrs and Prisoners Society. There, both groups used to meet in the same office, and that is how I met Hani, who was from my same city and our families were acquaintances.

"One day, Hani called me, handed me an envelope for safekeeping and told me: 'I am going on an assignment.' He instructed me to open it if he became martyred and to keep it closed if he returned safe. He was headed with a group of fighters on a military operation, and a few days later he returned, requested the envelope, and asked me out for a cup of coffee. At the time I refused to go with him.

"In the beginning of April 1970, he approached me again and we started seeing each other. We got married on July 24, 1970, and we lived on Al-Hayyek road (which leads to the First Circle in Jabal Amman). When the events of September broke out, I was unknowingly pregnant."

ESTABLISHING THE PHOTOGRAPHY DEPARTMENT
OF THE FATAH INFORMATION OFFICE

The nature of Sulafa and Hani's work at the Ministry of Information involved filming important events taking place in Jordan, like the activities of His Majesty the King, the government, and important figures in the country, in addition to covering important national celebrations like hosting guests and dignitaries and photographing military exercises and graduations ceremonies. The manager of the cinema department, Mr. Ali Siyam, would produce the Jordanian newsreels from this footage, which were screened at cinema houses (before the establishment of the Jordan Television at the end of 1967). A number of documentary films he produced were shot by Sulafa and Hani, including *The Exit*, *The Scorched Earth*, and *Zahrat al Mada'in* directed by Siyam, as well as the *Palestinian Right* directed by Mustafa Abu Ali in 1968.

Since joining Fatah, the three filmmakers thought about how they could serve the revolution through their work in cinema. The first step came when Sulafa suggested to the Fatah leadership, through her connection to one of the leaders, Abu Jihad,[21] that they establish a photography

---

[21] Abu Jihad, Khalil Al-Wazir, was a political and military leader, one of the founders and most prominent leaders who established the Fatah movement in the 1950s. He was a member of the central committee since its establishment, and he was the architect of the first Intifada that broke out in the Occupied Territories on December 9, 1987. He was assassinated by the Israeli Mossad on April 16, 1988.

department. She received approval, on the condition that they work with the existing space and equipment. This is where the three filmmakers began, and their slogan was, "Through the still and moving image we communicate and disseminate the concepts of the revolution to the people and ensure its continuity."

Hani's Account from "The First Beginnings"[22]

"We proceeded to work before we found the necessary space and equipment. Our work was limited, initially, to documenting photos of the martyrs and other jobs specific to the revolution. The Battle of Al-Karameh broke out on March 21, 1968, and the fedayeen of the Palestinian revolution stood their ground against the Israeli occupation army in a heroic battle that lasted 19 hours, until the Jordanian army was compelled to intervene alongside them. After the Battle of Al-Karameh, the revolution witnessed an outbreak of attention from international news agencies, and there was an urgent need for photographs. We were given a place to work, basically in the kitchen of one of the homes where all the revolution's operations gathered. The kitchen was transformed into a workshop for photography, developing, and printing images, as we worked with a simple camera and a basic drying device run on kerosene. The photography department started supplying the revolution's information office with photos of Palestinian events and the operations of the fedayeen, which were distributed to news agencies as the image of the Palestinian fedayeen started to take over the world."

Hani's Brother, Riyad Jawharieh's Memory[23]

"Hani photographed the whole fedayee mission in Al-Himmeh, north of Palestine towards the end of 1968 (Al-Himmeh is divided into three parts under Syrian, Jordanian, and Palestinian rule). The fedayeen reached the site through the Golan Heights, as they were led by the Lieutenant Nasr Youssef.[24] Hani accompanied the fighters who occupied Al-Himmeh for

---

[22] Hani Jawharieh, "The First Beginnings" republished in *Palestine in Cinema* (Ramallah: Ministry of Culture, 2006), p. 15–18.

[23] Riyad Jawharieh's recollections were given in an interview conducted by the author on October 25, 2016.

[24] Yousef Nasir, a Palestinian political and military leader, joined Fatah upon its establishment in 1965 while he was still a student. He joined the military wing Al Asifah and was elected a member of the central committee in the fifth congress in 1989.

Fig. 1.3   Sulafa Jadallah and Hani Jawharieh at Al-Karameh in March 1968

twelve hours, and they held a group of Israeli soldiers as hostages. However, they were unable to keep the hostages because the Israeli Air Force continued to circle the sky above them, forcing them to retreat and leave the hostages behind (Figs. 1.3 and 1.4).

"Abu Jihad trusted Hani and the photography department. He used to visit them for safety and rest. He would sometimes meet with the groups organizing in the West Bank in the photography department. It is said that Abu Jihad got hold of maps indicating the location of the Hawk Missile in Israel to prepare for a military operation. He wanted to photograph a map quickly so it could be returned to the Library of Congress before its disappearance was detected (it was obtained through a Palestinian student studying in America). When he sent it to Hani to photograph, Hani determined that their photography equipment was insufficient to capture it. He argued that it required lenses and equipment unavailable to them, and he referred Abu Jihad to his friend who was an Armenian photographer residing in Beirut. Sure enough, the maps were sent and photographed, and the originals were returned within three days."

Fig. 1.4 Sulafa Jadallah and Mustafa Abu Ali at Al-Karameh after the battle in March 1968

BIBLIOGRAPHY

Chmait, Walid and Guy Hennebelle, eds. *Filastin fi al-Sinima [Palestine in Cinema]*, 2nd ed. Ramallah: Wizarat al-Thaqafah al-Filastiniyah, al-Hay'ah al-'Ammah al-Filastiniyah lil Kitab, 2006.

Al-Najjar, Tayseer. Interview with Mustafa Abu Ali. Source uncertain, possibly *Al Arab Al Yaum* in Jordan, date NA, possibly late 1990s.

Al-Shayeb, Yousef. Interview with Mustafa Abu Ali. *Al-Ayyam* newspaper, August 4, 2009.

CHAPTER 2

Development of the Photography Department

After the Battle of Al-Karameh at the beginning of 1968, there was an explosion of news interest from the Arab countries and around the world. The press wanted to follow what happened in the battle where the fedayeen not only staunchly resisted the Israeli military apparatus but were also able to incur major damage to their ranks. Following the Jordanian army's support of the fedayeen, the Israeli troops were forced to withdraw, leaving some of their machinery behind on the battlefield.

As a result, the need for photography and documentation increased, as there was a great demand for images of the fedayeen, their military operations, and the revolution leadership. In turn, the photography department needed more photographers to cover the unfolding events. The department [Sulafa, Mustafa, Hani] approached the revolution's leadership asking for support from fighters who were interested in or had some experience in photography who could be trained to work in the photography department.

© The Author(s), under exclusive license to Springer Nature Switzerland AG 2023
K. Habashneh, *Knights of Cinema*, Palgrave Studies in Arab Cinema, https://doi.org/10.1007/978-3-031-18858-9_2

NABIL MAHDI TELLS THE STORY OF MUTEE'S INVOLVEMENT
WITH THE PHOTOGRAPHY DEPARTMENT[1]

Nabil Mahdi was born in the town of 'Azoun in the governorate of Qalqilyah in 1942. He completed his primary studies in 'Azoun then moved to Qalqilyah to complete his secondary studies. After that, he left to attend the University of Damascus but was assigned to teach in Algeria before completing his university studies. Toward the end of 1965, he joined Fatah, which had an office in Algeria headed by Khalil al-Wazir, known as Abu Jihad, one of the leaders of Fatah. He continued teaching until after the 1967 war, when Palestinian teachers (from among the 4000 in Algeria) were asked to attend military training camps at Blida.

The training was supposed to last six months, but there were delays in the sessions due to poor organization, and people were asked to return to their jobs. However, there remained behind around 100 men who joined Fatah, including Ribhi Al-Karameh (Ribhi Mohammad Hussein),[2] William Nassar,[3] Mustafa Wafi,[4] and a group of young men coming from Germany.

After that, Nabil and Mustafa Wafi returned to Damascus, carrying with them a letter for the brother Abu Ali Eyad (Walid Ahmad Nimr Al-Nimr),[5] allowing them to join the training session at Maysaloun with 400–500 other young men from Kuwait at the end of 1967, including Mutee' and Abu Thareef.

---

[1] Interview with Nabil Mahdi (real name: Mahmoud Majd) conducted by the author on June 20, 2017.

[2] Ribhi Mohammad Hussein (Ribhi Al-Karameh) was a fighter who quit his studies in Germany to join Fatah. He was nicknamed Ribhi Al-Karameh due to his heroic sacrifice in the Battle of Al-Karameh on March 21, 1968. During the battle, Ribhi blew himself up, along with a number of fighters, exploding an Israeli military tank as it drove over a trench advancing towards fedayeen targets. The operation barred the advancement of the tanks along the battlefield, contributing to the development of the battle in favor of the revolution.

[3] William Nassar was a political and military fighter who joined Fatah from its very beginning. He conducted several operations in the Occupied Territories and was detained in the occupation prisons from 1968 to 1982, eventually released in a prisoner's exchange. He was an academic researcher and writer and recently passed away on June 6, 2019, after a long battle with illness.

[4] Mustafa Wafi, a Palestinian teacher who worked in the education sector in Algeria, joined Fateh in its early days, becoming the head of the Fatah office in Algeria.

[5] Walid Ahmad Al-Nimr, famously known as Abu Ali Eyad, was a Fateh military leader who also joined the movement in its very beginnings. He was a member of the first central committee and was responsible for the fighter training camps. He was martyred, after refusing to withdraw from the Battle of the Jerash Forests in 1971.

Nabil and Mutee' became friends after joining the Al-Himmeh and Maysaloun camps for fedayeen training in Syria and were transferred together to the bases in the Jordan Valley after the Battle of Al-Karameh. This is how he describes Mutee' joining the photography department.

"One day, Abu Jihad arrived on the base and asked the trainer, Saeed, if there were any fighters who had experience or interest in photography, explaining that the photography department was recruiting young men. The trainer led him to the fighter Mutee', who used to own a photography studio in Kuwait. Abu Jihad, who was happy to find a fighter experienced in photography, went looking for Mutee'.

"Abu Jihad said, 'Al-Hamdulillah I have found you, brother Mutee'! The guys at the photography department will be very pleased that you join them. They have a lot of work and the demand for photographs has increased tremendously after Al-Karameh Battle. They can't meet all the requests.'

"Mutee' replied, 'I am sorry, brother Abu Jihad. I left the photography studio in Kuwait and joined the training camps to fight with my fedayee brothers, not to be photographer.'

"Abu Jihad: 'But, brother Mutee', photography is as important to us as fighting because it disseminates our image to the world. To be honest, we have many fighters, but only three photographers, and they can no longer meet the increasing demand for photos of the fedayeen and the revolution activities.'

"But, Mutee' remained adamant in his opinion and refused to move from the military base to the photography department. A number of fighters from the base intervened to try to convince Mutee' to move.

"After some back-and-forth debates, he said, 'I will not transfer from here before I participate in a military operation against Israel.'

"Abu Jihad replied, 'Ok, brother Mutee', I promise that you will be involved in the first operation that heads to the occupied lands.'

"This is how Mutee' agreed to transfer to the photography department after Abu Jihad promised to allow him to participate in a military operation."

Amneh Naser Summarizes Husband Mutee's[6] Background

"Mutee' was born in 1942 in the village of Raimoun, district of Ramallah, the son of Dar Naser from Al-Shoufah tribe. He completed his secondary studies at Al-Husain College in Amman, where he earned the Matric degree. He was enthusiastic about photography which he pursued through training workshops. He later moved to Kuwait and opened a studio there. After the events of the 1967 war, he joined Fatah, and went to the Maysaloun and Al-Himmeh camps at the end of 1967 where he trained. He then joined the fedayee bases in the Jordan Valley."

Nabil Continues (from Previously Referenced Testimony)[7]

"On June 28, 1968 I took part in one of the fedayee operations in the middle strip.[8] The group was comprised of seven fighters, four of whom were injured. It was the first operation where injured fighters were able to return with their weapons. After I left the hospital, during the six-month recovery period I spent at the rehabilitation house, I used to visit the photography department to spend time with my friend Mutee' whom I had met at Al-Himmeh training camp. I used to help them with the required work like drying the photographs. But, I remained a fighter and didn't join the photography department even though I had worked with them for a long time."

Sulafa and Hani Resign from the Jordanian Ministry of Information to Dedicate Themselves Full-Time to the Photography Department

At the beginning of 1969, during the planning period for the first photography exhibition commemorating the anniversary of the Battle of Al-Karameh, Sulafa and Hani each felt the importance of dedicating

---

[6] Interview with Amneh Naser, the widow of the martyr Mutee' (real name: Ibrahim Mustafa Naser), conducted by the author on September 24, 2017.

[7] Interview with Nabil Mahdi (real name: Mahmoud Majd) conducted by the author on June 20, 2017.

[8] The "middle strip" is both a PLO military designation for a geographic area in the middle of Palestine and a wing within Fatah. This term "middle strip" is also used in south Lebanon, among Fatah fighters' bases.

themselves, full-time, to the photography department. Sulafa submitted her resignation to the Jordanian Ministry of Information, and Hani followed soon after, as he felt the pressure of the work required. The Ministry of Information agreed to Hani's resignation on March 16, 1969 because of his insistence. He had completed or was close to completing the service time required for recipients of the scholarship through the ministry. This is how Hani and Sulafa freed themselves to work at the photography department.

AL-KARAMEH EXHIBITION: THE FIRST WORK
OF THE PHOTOGRAPHY DEPARTMENT

Occasionally I would accompany Mustafa on his afternoon visits to the photography department when it was in the valley separating Jabal Amman and Jabal Al-Waibdeh, where Wadi Saqra Street currently stands.

One day in March 1969, we went there while they were working on enlarging photos of fedayeen and placing them on reinforced cardboard. I volunteered to help. Immediately, Hani instructed, as he handed me a paintbrush, "Here you go, spread the glue on the wooden board, Mutee' and I will hold the photo from both sides to stick it in place."

This was the first task I did with the group. I was happy to help, though modestly, in preparing for the first Al-Karameh exhibition which took place at Al-Wihdat camp and proved to be very successful.[9]

This Al-Karameh exhibition of March 1969 was among the most important achievements of the photography department at that time. The preparation for the exhibition brought together a small number of revolutionaries who contributed, day and night, in good team spirit, to gather all the necessary work. This included everything from developing, printing, enlarging, and gluing photographs to hammering nails to hang the works.

Huge photographs of the fedayeen were exhibited in several conjoined tents at Al-Wihdat camp. This was the first time the Palestinian people saw their own image that spoke of their cause and their revolution through

[9] Al-Wihdat camp is one of the largest Palestinian refugee camps in Jordan. It was established after the Nakba in 1955 on the eastern edge of Amman. Over time, it has transformed into a large neighborhood, considered to be one of the most commercially active districts in the Jordanian capital, Amman.

their own sons, the fighters. Though the exhibition relied initially on still photographs, some Arab artists participated by offering artworks expressing the Palestinian Revolution. Among them, I recall the Palestinian artist Mustafa Al-Hallaj,[10] the Syrian artists Nazir Naba'a, the incredible fine artist and calligrapher Mustafa Arna'out, and three Egyptian artists: fine artist and caricaturist Bahgat Al-Bahgoury, alongside caricaturists Bahjat Othman and Mohammad Haqqi. They were accompanied by the militant journalist Ahmad Al-Azhari.[11]

The exhibition was favorably received, and the success it garnered was unprecedented. It traveled to various other places and countries and its triumph played a huge role in the development of the photography department. The success brought new, modern equipment and later helped to recruit several fighters after the Palestinian image became an important weapon in the revolution's arsenal (Fig. 2.1).

However, the joy of the photography guys, as they were known, was short-lived. While they were preparing for the Al-Karameh exhibition, Sulafa was tragically shot and sustained a head injury. This was a major blow because she was the group's cornerstone and main organizer.

Abdelraheem Jadallah, Sulafa's Youngest Brother, Narrates the Story of Her Injury[12]

"In March 1969, as the film guys were preparing for the exhibition commemorating the first anniversary of Al-Karameh Battle, Sulafa was inadvertently wounded in the head while shooting.

"Her colleagues rushed her to Al-Ashrafiyeh hospital, but because there was no doctor specialized in neuroscience, all they did was try to stop the bleeding, nothing else. Some of the doctors even told us to leave her, that

---

[10] Mustafa Al-Hallaj was one of the first Palestinian fine artists. He developed a prominent school of Palestinian and Arab fine arts, and was a friend of the Palestine Film Unit, participating in some of its works. He died in a tragic accident, burning in the studio where he lived and worked in Damascus in 2002.

[11] Ahmad Al-Azhari, whose real name is Farouq Al-Qadi, was a well-known leftist Egyptian author and journalist who joined Fatah in 1968. He worked as the head of press and external relations with the Soviet bloc and socialist countries. He also worked as the legal advisor and head of Yasser Arafat's office in the beginning of the 1970s.

[12] Abdelraheem's narration is from the written interview conducted by the author on February 27, 2018.

Poster by Mustafa al-Hallaj for the 1969 exhibit commemorating the Battle of Karamah.
Courtesy of the Palestine Poster Project Archive.

Fig. 2.1 Poster of Al-Karameh Exhibition by the fine artist Mustafa Al Hallaj

there was no chance she would survive. When Abu Ammar,[13] may God bless his soul, heard of this, he came to the hospital immediately to check on her state. He was deeply worried by her condition and asked King Hussein to move her to the Jordanian Military Hospital in Marka. He also demanded that she receive the attention of a specialized doctor from Jerusalem. By the time the specialized doctor arrived, parts of her brain were already damaged, and she had undergone numerous surgeries. At the hospital, she was accompanied by the sisters Hind Jawharieh and Ihsan Bernawi.[14] Alhamdullilah, thank God, her condition started to improve, but there were long term effects because she was partially paralyzed. Despite this, she maintained her strong faith and willpower during the surgery as she did not stop thanking God and reciting verses from the Quran. Because she needed to stay close to the military hospital in Marka where she received continuous physical therapy, we moved to North Marka to be close to her.

"After that, the leader Abu Ammar ordered that Sulafa be sent to Hungary to undertake surgery to patch her skull which was cracked. Our colleague Hind Jawharieh accompanied her on this trip. Despite this long phase Sulafa did not surrender to her condition and continued to fight with all her ability and energy. Her perseverance and steadfastness shocked the Hungarian doctors. After her surgery and recovery, which lasted about three months, she returned to Amman."

Eram Jadallah, Sulafa's Brother, Recalls Sulafa[15]

"Sulafa documented, with Hani, the displacement of families crossing the [Allenby] bridge, and she participated in capturing images of the Green Belt operation in 1967. She also photographed the Israeli soldier who stayed in the tank at Al-Karameh, and [later] when she was hit by a bullet, he suspected that the Israelis planted someone to shoot her."

---

[13] Abu Ammar (real name: Yasser Arafat) was a founding member of Fatah and head of its central committee since its establishment. A political and military leader, he headed the Palestine Liberation Organization (PLO) since its establishment in 1969 and the Palestinian National Authority after the return of PLO to the Occupied Territories in 1994. He was elected president in 1996 and remained in power until his assassination in 2004.

[14] Ihsan Bernawi, a militant woman who joined Fatah in its early stages, was a resident of Jerusalem and was forced to leave for Jordan to avoid being imprisoned after her participation in a military operation.

[15] Eram Jadallah's testimony was obtained in an interview conducted by the author on June 23, 2018.

Naseef[16] Joins the Photography Department

Naseef was born in 1946 in the village of Al-Tireh, in the district of Ramleh and Al-Lydd. He fled with his family when he was two years old and completed his primary and middle school education in Amman at Al-Wihdat camp. He left school after the eleventh grade and received the Tawjeehi (secondary school degree) through private studying. Then, he worked at studio Albair Flouti in Amman, as he was interested in photography, and after that at Studio Hanna Salameh, until he got the chance to work as a photographer contracted by a studio in Saudi Arabia. He came on vacation from Saudi Arabia in August 1967, but remained and opened his own small shop, which he kept for some time.

Naseef recalls, "After the events of February 1969,[17] in the middle of the year, I joined the fedayeen and worked for a while with the military police." Motivated by his interest and experience in photography, Naseef requested to be moved to the photography department at the Fatah Information Office. Hani interviewed him and tested his photography skills before accepting him and assigning him to the photography department that was in Wadi Saqra near Jabal Amman. While there, he learned of Sulafa's incident that had occurred a month or two before he joined, and he met Mutee', Mustafa, and then Nabil who joined the department on Mutee's recommendation.

The photographers used to accompany some military operations and produced photographic surveys of enemy outposts through coordination with Abu Sabri[18] or Abu Jihad (member of Fatah's Central Committee/ Military Wing). In addition, they photographed the training camps, and all the activities and events organized by the revolution, including conferences, festivals, and protests. They also prepared photography exhibitions about the revolution for use in the country and to accompany delegations traveling abroad.

---

[16] This recollection by Naseef (real name: Adil al-Kesbeh) was given in an interview at Adil Studio in Al-Wihdat camp conducted by the author on June 27, 2014.

[17] The first clashes occurred late 1969 between a group from the Jordanian army and a group of fedayeen. Through the joint effort of the Palestinian and Jordanian leadership, the clash was quickly contained and halted.

[18] Abu Sabri (real name: Mamdouh Saydam) was a military leader and member of the Central Committee of Fatah. He joined the movement before it was launched, and was chosen deputy director of military operations for Al-'Asifah forces after his participation in the Battle of Beit Furik in 1967 where he was the commander of the area of Jenin. He died from terminal illness in 1971.

By mid-1969, there was great pressure on the department from the increased demand for images and Sulafa's absence. A group of around ten fighters was invited to join them, and a training workshop was conducted for the fighters, but ultimately only two fighters ended up joining: Abu Thareef, and Omar. The rest were considered correspondents and liaisons with the fedayee bases.

NABIL REMEMBERS SOME FIGHTERS WHO JOINED THE PHOTOGRAPHY DEPARTMENT[19]

"Naseef had been part of the military police before he joined around mid-1969, shortly after Sulafa's accident. And as I recall, Omar and Abu Thareef enlisted in the second half, or at the end of 1969. Hani and Naseef trained them with nine to ten other young men, brought together from various bases to receive photography training. However, only Omar and Abu Thareef remained. Omar had been working in Kuwait and joined the revolution and participated in missile training in Cairo. As for Abu Thareef, he was, as I recall, from Dara'a camp and was a friend of mine from Al-Himmeh base, which is what motivated him to join the photography department. We used to shoot at the beginning without any real technical or artistic training in photography. The photographers would follow the events to cover them, and when one or two would leave to take the pictures, we'd always say, 'Take care of the film.'"

Nabil continues: "Despite this [the fact that they were in the process of training], Fouad Al-Tuhami, well-known Egyptian film director, remembers the shot of the fedayee as he jumps over a flame, and the image of the Israeli war planes during the 1973 war, that were shot by Mutee', remarking, 'This photographer deserves a medal.'"

ABU THAREEF[20]

Abu Thareef was born in the village of Zayta, in the district of Toulkarem, in 1942. He fled with his family to Syria in 1948, where he studied and enrolled in a vocational training program to learn surveying, the field he

---

[19] Nabil's recollections were shared in the second interview conducted by the author on June 27, 2017.

[20] This testimony by Abu Thareef (real name: Tawfiq Musa Khalil) was given in an interview conducted by the author on August 15, 2016.

would continue to work in. His hobby was music and he received training in playing the oud. Once he tried to build an oud by himself.

Abu Thareef returned to Nablus in 1960 to receive a Jordanian passport allowing him to travel to Kuwait. There, he worked as a surveyor and met Mutee' (Ibrahim Naser) and Omar (Abdelhafeth Al-Asmar) through his visits with Omar to the studio where Mutee' worked. While in Kuwait, they met many members of Fatah, and joined its organization.

After the 1967 war they joined the Fatah training camps in Damascus and trained with Al-Sai'ka. It is here that he met the brother Nabil who had also joined the camp and was learning to build explosive weapons, having completed his military training in Algeria. After the battle of Al-Karameh they headed to the fedayee bases in the mountains of Al-Salt in Jordan.

Abu Thareef recalls that after a short period at the base, around mid-1968, Abu Jihad arrived and asked Mutee' to join the photography department after learning about his previous experience. Abu Thareef joined the department after more than a year, in the second half of 1969.

Enayah Abu Awn, Widow of Omar Al-Mukhtar (Real Name Abdelhafeth Al-Asmar) Recalls[21]

Omar was born in Turmus Ayya in 1942 and was educated in Ramallah where he received his Tawjihi (secondary school) certificate. His mother passed away when he was twelve years old, and he was raised with his two brothers and sister by their paternal aunt and grandmother. He worked for a short while at the postal service until he moved to Kuwait, where he also worked in the postal service. There, he joined the Fatah movement, but after the 1967 war, as fedayee work spread, he moved to their militant branch.

Omar was transferred at the end of 1969 to work with the photography department of the Fatah Information Office, where he received training in photography from Hani Jawharieh (Fig. 2.2).

"These are the events that shaped the beginnings of the Photography Department, and the people who joined it as a continuation of their involvement with the Palestinian Revolution."

---

[21] Enaya Abu Awn, Omar Al Mukhtar's widow, told his life story in an interview conducted by the author on September 28, 2017.

Fig. 2.2   Mutee' and Abu Thareef (in the middle) among the fighters, 1968

BIBLIOGRAPHY

Interview with Enaya Abu Awn conducted by the author at Sep 28th, 2017.
Interview with Naseef (Adil al Kesbeh) conducted by the author on June 27th, 2014.
Interview with Abdelraheem Jadallah conducted by the author on February 27th, 2018.
Interview with Eram Jadallah conducted by the author on June 23rd, 2018.
Interview with Nabil Mahdi conducted by the author on June 20, 2017.
Interview with Amneh Naser conducted by the author on September 24th, 2017.
Interview with Abu Thareef conducted by the author on August 15th, 2016.

CHAPTER 3

Creation of the Palestine Film Unit

In 1968, the filmmakers Sulafa, Hani, and Mustafa started thinking about cinematically documenting the events and activities of the revolution using a borrowed camera, without a clear plan. They called this work the Palestine Film Unit (PFU).

Mustafa's Recollections About the Origins of the PFU

At the end of 1968, the Palestine Film Unit (PFU) was established, and it belonged to the Fatah movement. It was the first filmmaking unit to work within an armed Palestinian organization. The unit started its work in photographing and filming the popular events of the Palestinian revolution after the Battle of Al-Karameh when there was a huge popular interest in the revolution.

Mustafa explained their objectives as follows: "Thinking that important events were unfolding in the region that need to be documented and preserved until the right time comes to benefit from the footage. In addition to documenting popular events, the military activities of the Palestinian revolution in Jordan, Syria and Lebanon were filmed."

Mustafa clarified later in the same interview: "after acquiring an Arriflex film camera and Nagra sound recorder towards the end of 1969, the film

© The Author(s), under exclusive license to Springer Nature Switzerland AG 2023
K. Habashneh, *Knights of Cinema*, Palgrave Studies in Arab Cinema, https://doi.org/10.1007/978-3-031-18858-9_3

unit was able to complete its first documentary film *No to a Peaceful Solution*.[1] The unit continued its important work at this time and developed the richest cinematic and photographic archive of the contemporary Palestinian Revolution."

I personally remember during that time the unit receiving as a gift two 16 mm projectors and a number of films about other popular struggles. The beginning of the cinematic movement screened these films at the fedayee bases in the Jordan Valley and Southern Lebanon, and in the camps. These screenings were met with a lot of excitement and enthusiasm, as it was the first time we were able to bring the experiences of other popular struggles to our people and our militants. I still recall screening the Vietnamese film *Dushka Women Throwers* at the Complex of Syndicates in Amman. Fatah mobilized many of its members and cadres to attend the event and the Fatah Women's Office[2] relied on it in their call for greater support for establishing a female militia.

Beginning with *No to a Peaceful Solution*

Director Salah Abu Hannoud Joins the Palestine Film Unit

I had previously met Salah Abu Hannoud through our membership in the Jordanian theatre troupe. We were colleagues who shared an educational specialization in psychology and an interest in theatre.

Salah was born in Asireh, in the district of Nablus, in 1944. He completed his secondary education in Nablus and received a BA in psychology from the University of Jordan in 1967. He was a theatre enthusiast and participated in several plays and productions throughout secondary school and university. He joined the first Jordanian theatre troupe when it was established in 1965 by theatre director Hani Snowbar.

---

[1] When this film screened in France in the early 1970s it was called *No to Roger's Plan*.

[2] The Women's Office worked on the empowerment of women and their roles in the underground political organization of Fatah. It is a prominent part of the General Union of Palestinian Women (GUPW), which is an open popular union actively working among all Palestinian women for social and political mobilization to raise awareness about women's issues and provide training courses to raise standards of living, among other things. The GUPW belongs to the PLO and is led by an elected executive committee from most Palestinian political organizations that are affiliated with the PLO.

Salah Speaks About His Relationship with the Palestine Film Unit[3]

"At the beginning of 1968, I got a job at the Jordan Television as an assistant director for a short while. I was sent for training in film production for three months in London in mid-1968, then returned to work as an assistant director. Later I met with brother Nazeh Abu Nidal[4] who tried to recruit me to join Fatah, however I wasn't enthusiastic about political or military work. So Abu Nidal suggested that I meet Mustafa Abu Ali who worked in cinema. I used to know Hani and Mustafa through my involvement in theatre at the culture and arts department of the Ministry of Information, as they worked in the cinema department on the first floor of the Ministry. The first work I was involved in was accompanying Hani Jawharieh when he filmed a popular mass march rejecting the Rogers Peace Plan."[5]

Salah Describes His Experience with the film No to a Peaceful Solution[6]

"The most important thing I remember about the film was the conversations that we had with Mustafa and Hani around how to make a film that expresses the revolution in a militant, and non-bourgeois way, and we started thinking about how we would express peoples' anger and rejection of the Rogers Plan. We filmed the young lions (Al-Ashbal) training, the fedayee bases and several activities and events of the revolution like the workshops of the Sons of the Martyrs Society and the Palestinian Red Crescent. The film's plan, as I recall, was as follows: the three of us decided to include parallel shots of the march, the trainings and operations of the

---

[3] Interview with the director Salah Abu Hannoud on September 25, 2015, conducted by the author.

[4] Nazeh Abu Nidal (real name: Ghattas Swaiss), a militant in Fatah movement, was a journalist and political delegate among the militants. He was from a Jordanian family based in the town of Al-Fuhais.

[5] A popular mass march, launched to express the people's and leadership's anger and rejection of the political initiative known as the Rogers Plan. The Rogers Plan addressed the results of the June 1967 War, where Israel occupied additional Palestinian and Arab lands, but ignored the Palestinian Revolution and the Palestine Liberation Organization (PLO).

[6] Salah Abu Hannoud's interview with the author conducted on September 25, 2015.

fedayeen, and some events and activities of the revolution, accompanied by segments of revolutionary songs and chants. When we started thinking of a name or title for the film, we agreed it would also need to be a revolutionary name. At first, we decided on *The Armed People's Revolution Says: No to the Peaceful Solution.*"

"When we started planning around travel to Studio Ba'albak in Beirut to work on editing the film there, Mustafa quickly suggested that I go, and this is what happened. I travelled to Beirut with our brother Sakher Habash, and I edited the film as we had agreed in Amman. We were captivated by the idea of making a revolutionary militant film to the extent that we kept entire rushes without removing the slightest detail, not even the black frames that appear at the end of a shot.

"We decided that the work was undertaken collaboratively, without naming specific people, such that it was a revolutionary work. I will never forget the enthusiasm and excitement with which the film was received, especially when we screened it at the annual conference of the Union of Palestinian Students held at the Islamic College in mid-1970.

"I worked with Mustafa and Hani throughout Black September 1970, and I used to sometimes stay overnight at the department's headquarters in Jabal Al-Jofeh. I met Abu Ammar who would occasionally come and sleep there and I recall that he would prepare breakfast for the photography guys himself. In this period, I also met the rest of the photography department team, Mutee', Omar, Abu Thareef, Nabil and Naseef. When the Arab Summit Conference convened in Cairo over the events of Black September, we gathered photographic material of the events for Abu Ammar to take and show to the Arab leaders." (Figs. 3.1 and 3.2).

"Abu Ammar suggested that the name 'Palestine Films' should be added to *The Armed People's Revolution Says: No to the Peaceful Solution* when he found no names on the film."

Hani Discusses the First Film in His Article "The First Beginnings"

"At the end of 1968, we started our limited cinematic activities by borrowing a 16 mm film camera to document Palestinian events including

Fig. 3.1 Abu Ammar in the Photography Department at Jabal Al-Jofeh during Black September of 1970, carrying baby Sulafa, Mutee's daughter, and behind him Salah Abu Hanoud. Mutee' and his wife, who came for a visit, couldn't return home because of the intensive shelling

Fig. 3.2 The first logo of the Palestine Film Unit

military operations, press conferences, and protests. We didn't have a specific plan in place at the beginning, but we were acutely aware of the revolution's need for documenting its struggle and the peoples' engagement with this struggle. In 1969, the department received a more advanced film camera with additional equipment, an audio recorder, and other equipment that allowed for executing the work in difficult circumstances and with higher quality.

"Then, we started thinking about a cinematic production plan in service of the revolution. The first Palestinian film produced was called *No to a Peaceful Solution* and it captured the reactions of the Palestinian leadership and masses to the Rogers Plan at the end of 1969. The film was first screened in the presence of a group of the revolution's leadership in an underground shelter on a floor littered with sand and rubble. The audience watched the film while standing but their gaze followed every shot with keen interest even though many artistic aspects of the film were below standards because of the speed with which it was completed."[7]

The film became the actual beginning of the Palestine Film Unit.

International Film Groups and the Palestinian Revolution

In 1969 and 1970, the Palestinian revolution and Palestine Film Unit welcomed several news agencies and filmmaking crews from Italy, France, the United States, and elsewhere. They were attracted by the image of the fedayeen, which became famous after the Battle of Al-Karameh and the steadfastness of the Palestinian fighters against the Israeli Occupation forces. Among them was News Real, a radical group from the United States who filmed a documentary in the beginning of 1970 entitled *Revolution Until Victory*, echoing one of Fatah's slogans. The film was about the Zionist movement's plans, the beginnings of the Palestinian issue, and the reasons behind the launch of the Palestinian Revolution. The group later provided the PFU with an original copy of the film (a dupe negative), which it considered to be a joint production because of the services and assistance offered to them.

The Italian director Luigi Perelli also arrived and made a film entitled *Al-Fatah*, produced by the Italian Communist Party in 1970. The PFU

---

[7] Hani Jawharieh, "The First Beginnings" republished in *Palestine in Cinema* (Ramallah: Ministry of Culture, 2006), p. 15–18.

received an original copy of this film as well in appreciation of the help and production services offered to the film crew.

A number of filmmakers were hosted by leftist Palestinian organizations, like the Popular Front for the Liberation of Palestine (PFLP) and the Democratic Front for the Liberation of Palestine (DFLP). Among them was the Japanese director Koji Wakamatsu who filmed and directed the work *United Red Army/and PFLP: Declaration of World War*, where he followed the Popular Front's operation of exploding the hijacked plane with support from the Japanese Red Army right before the onset of the events of Black September.

The Italian director Ugo Adilardi, who was a member of the Italian Communist Party, also came, and he directed a film entitled *The Long March of Return* in collaboration with the DFLP.

Among the most important figures who came to Jordan during this period was the French director Jean-Luc Godard, who was among the ten most important directors in the world in the 1960s. He was an avant-garde filmmaker, who had supported the 1968 student revolution in France, followed the events of Czechoslovakia, made a film about workers in Italy and Britain, and in 1969 started considering making a film about the Palestinian Revolution.

When Mahmoud Al-Hamshari,[8] the head of the Palestine Office in Paris, learned of this, he asked Elias Sanbar,[9] an active member among the Palestinian Students Union leadership in Paris, to make arrangements to support Godard's trip. Elias accompanied Godard on his visits to Jordan and Lebanon to meet with the fighters at the bases and the leaders of the revolution. Mustafa accompanied Godard on his visits to all the sites, to the interviews with fighters at the bases, and with members of the political leadership.

[8] Mahmoud Al-Hamshari, one of the political and diplomatic leaders of Fatah, was the first head of the Palestine office in France and is considered among the architects of Palestinian diplomatic work. He was assassinated by the Israeli Mossad and martyred on January 10, 1973.

[9] Interview with Elias Sanbar, conducted by the author in Paris, March 12, 2018. A member of the Palestinian Students Union leadership in France in the 1960s, Sanbar is currently the Palestinian ambassador to the United Nations Educational, Scientific and Cultural Organization (UNESCO).

JEAN-LUC GODARD VISITS THE PALESTINIAN REVOLUTION

During his time with the Palestinian Revolution, Godard frequently visited the Information Office of Fatah, with whom he chose to make his film. He mentioned this in a statement published in the Fatah newspaper at the beginning of 1970, which he introduced as follows:

> As revolutionaries in the field of cinema, the current task upon us remains theoretical. We are in the stage where we believe that thinking differently produces the revolution. In this, we are decades behind the first bullet fired by Al-'Asifah (the military wing of Fatah).

The long statement that follows includes several excerpts under the following headings: "Political Front and Artistic Front," "The Bullet Near the Ear," "Relations Between Images", "The Agents of Hollywood," "Thoughts and Contradictions," and "Teeth and Lips."

Godard Discusses "The Political Front and the Artistic Front"

"We came here to study, learn and draw lessons. If we can record lessons, we will later publish them here or there or anywhere in the world. Last year, two of our colleagues joined to conduct an investigation: one with the Democratic Front for the Liberation of Palestine and the other with Fatah. We read the texts and programs given. We found the political discussions with the comrades of the DFLP are almost like the discussions with our comrades in Paris: we didn't learn from them, and they didn't learn from us. But with Fatah fedayee and militants it was different: we heard something new that we can learn from. As we are French Maoists we decided to work on a film with Fatah which we initially called *Until Victory*. We left the Palestinians to utter the word 'revolution' during the film, but the real name of the film is 'the intellectual curriculum and work of the Palestinian National Liberation Movement (Fatah).'"

An Excerpt from "Relations Between Images"

"The film needs to be useful in the short run and the long run ... let us take an example: an image of a fedayee crossing the river, then an image of a militant woman from Fatah teaching reading and writing to women in a Palestinian refugee camp, then an image of a shibel (young lion) training.

What do these images mean? These three images separately are not important. They may have emotional or photographic value, but individually, they do not have political value. To obtain a political meaning, each one of these images needs to be linked to the two other images. In this moment, what becomes important is the order in which the images appear, for it represents the political trajectory which gives images their political meaning. We follow Fatah's trajectory, and as such, we order the images as follows, (1) fedayee in an operation, (2) a militant woman teaches reading, (3) children training. This means (1) armed struggle, (2) political work, (3) long term popular war. The third image is the culmination of the first and the second image. Armed struggle plus political work equals long term popular war against Israel."

Godard Continues with "Thoughts and Contradictions"

"Our task now, as revolutionaries in the field of anti-imperialist media, is to resist with all our power in this field, and to liberate ourselves from the chain of images imposed on us by imperialist ideology through its various apparatuses, from newspapers to broadcast to cinema films, books, etc."[10] (Fig. 3.3)

Mustafa Abu Ali's Perception of Godard's Visit

In excerpts from an interview with Tayseer Al-Najjar, Mustafa reflected: "The famous French director Jean-Luc Godard came to Amman to make a film about the Palestinian Revolution ... I used to accompany him on almost all his trips. He carried more or less the same preoccupation I carried, which is the search for a militant or revolutionary cinema. Godard deepened my concerns, and added new questions to my inquiries, which all revolved around mechanisms for developing a militant Palestinian cinema."[11]

Mustafa continued later in the interview:

Godard brought with him revolutionary ideas about cinema which we discussed often. The ideas he posed were close to what I was preoccupied with,

[10] Walid Chmait and Guy Hennebelle, *Palestine in Cinema* (Ramallah: Palestinian Ministry of Culture, 2006), p. 262–268.
[11] Interview by journalist Tayseer Al-Najjar, found among Mustafa's archive, typed on A4 papers, with no publishing date or newspaper, assumed to be conducted in the late 1990s. Al-Najjar used to write for *Al-Arab Al-Yawm* (*The Arab Today*).

Fig. 3.3 Jean-Luc Godard filming at Al Baqa' camp near Amman, photographed by Mustafa Abu Ali, 1969

but the ongoing question always remained how those ideas can be implemented and embodied in film. I suppose Godard also encountered the same question. By accompanying him throughout his time shooting the film, I noticed his frustrations and hesitations multiple times, as I encountered his cinematic genius on all occasions.

Hassan Abu Ghanimeh adds to this from his book, *About the Palestinian Cinema* (1975): "At the beginning of 1970, Godard had already made three revolutionary films about workers in Italy, workers in Britain, and the third about events in Czechoslovakia which was, according to him, a mistake because it relied on faulty political analysis. When he came to Jordan, he tried to draw on his experience from the first three films in his film about the Palestinian revolution.

Godard's mission was also similar to our commitment within the Palestine Film Unit. Although the unit was not in complete agreement with him, we eagerly awaited the results, anxious to see how the theory would be implemented at the level of cinematic practice. For various reasons, the unit had not yet seen the film until now."[12]

Godard's film was later produced under the title *Here and Elsewhere* in 1976, and it provoked a wide debate among filmmakers.

In another excerpt from the interview with Al-Najjar, Mustafa discusses cinematic style:

> In this framework where militant cinema remains a conceptual idea without a model to be replicated, my films are all considered to be experimental. If you watch them, you will not find a film that looks like another, because each has its own different style, but it also carries within it a piece of myself. This experimentation was my search for a militant cinema, a cinema that springs from our reality in this area.

Salah Abu Hanoud Recalls Godard's Visit

"Godard came, as I remember, at the end of 1969 or the beginning of 1970. Mustafa accompanied him most of the time, and occasionally Hani joined. Godard returned to Jordan again in mid-1970 before the events of Black September. I recall accompanying Godard and Mustafa to downtown Amman, upon Godard's request, to see advertisements of cinemas. Godard noticed that most of the advertisements were for war films, and he commented that the country is preparing for war. I remembered Godard's remark when Black September started as I was astonished by his prediction."[13]

My Memories of Godard

As Mustafa was accompanying Godard, he returned one day from one of their outings and said: "Godard wants to film a militant woman who can hardly read and write. Can you arrange that for him?"

I replied: "Yes. I will look at the schedule of the lessons at the Illiteracy Eradication center, and we'll choose a woman who recently joined the program."

---

[12] Mustafa Abu Ali and Hassan Abu Ghanimeh, *About the Palestinian Cinema* (Beirut: Palestine Film Unit, 1975), p. 27–28.

[13] Salah's recollection was obtained in an interview conducted by the author on September 25, 2015.

We ended up choosing a woman called Rabeeha, who had been among the last women to register for lessons.

When Godard arrived to shoot the scene, Rabeeha stood and read fluently. He lost hope, and so did we, because it became clear to us that this woman spent most of her time reading and studying what she learned in the literacy lessons. She had reached almost full fluency within an unexpected period of time.

Of course, we looked for another woman who fit Godard's need, someone who would express the beginning of the role of women in the revolution.

But what I distinctly remember about him was his odd behavior, consistent with the many things I had heard about him and his humorous responses to the revolution's political leadership.

Wherever he went, Godard took with him Mao Tse-tung's *Red Book*, which seemed to be his daily planner. I will never forget when we invited him to our house for dinner the day before he left. He looked around at the contents of our book shelves and found several books about him and his films. I was very surprised when he took them and threw them in the rubbish bin. When he watched the shocked expression on my face, he said, "This is bourgeois garbage…. All this technology on…" and he pointed toward his backside.

After the events of Black September, Godard stopped working on the completion of his film. Then he was involved in a big car accident that was widely reported in the newspapers. After recovering from the accident, he completed his film *Everything's Alright*.

We heard nothing more about *Until Victory*, until 1976, when he completed a very different film entitled *Here and Elsewhere*.

According to Guy Hennebelle, Godard presented in this film

> a number of important technical issues like the importance of sound and image, questioning which is more useful through his self-reflexive audio interventions that discuss and critique scenes of the film. The film also draws comparisons through oscillating between shots, for example of Jews in Israel and Jews at a Nazi concentration camp during the war, or between the life of a family living in France and a family living in Palestine, etc.

As mentioned, Godard's film ignited a wide debate among critics and filmmakers.

Hennebelle further critiqued the film as "simply stupid and useless." Hennebelle continued, "Some of my filmmaker friends like it, but I don't understand why! I personally believe that Godard has no right to make a film like this about an important and real issue like the Palestinian Revolution, for which many men and women have sacrificed their lives in relentless resistance."[14]

In reality, Godard expressed through this film philosophical ideas about the relationship between sound and image, and these ideas cannot be easily conveyed to an audience.

PERSISTING THROUGH THE EVENTS OF BLACK SEPTEMBER

Militant Naseef's Recollection

"At the beginning of 1970, and perhaps towards the end of 1969, the photography department moved to Jabal Al-Jofeh. During this period, I also met Salah Abu-Hannoud. The department's photographers covered the events of Black September by spreading around in several areas. I was covering Al-Wihdat."[15]

Abu Thareef Describes Black September

"During the events of Black September, we spread out to cover the clashes. I used to photograph in Al-Ashrafiyeh hospital, and downtown by the Arab Bank. Naseef was in Al-Wihdat and Mutee' was in Al-Ashrafiyeh hospital and other areas. We would return to the photography department in Al-Jofeh, and with us was Salah Abu-Hannoud. As for Mustafa and Hani, they covered events in various areas and were sometimes accompanied by Salah. After the events, we continued to work in the department, and we photographed some of the activities of the Arab Commission. After that, we accompanied the commission to Damascus, under the leadership of Al Bahi Ladgham,[16] leaving with the Palestinian leadership's bus and taking with us all our photography equipment. When we reached

---

[14] Hassan Abu Ghanimeh, *Palestine and the Cinematic Eye* (Damascus: Union of Arab Writers, 1981), p. 380.

[15] Naseef's recollections were gathered in the interview conducted by the author on June 27, 2014.

[16] Al Bahi Ladgham, a high-ranking Libyan military official, came as a head of a commission of Arab leaders, nominated from the Arab summit held in Cairo to stop the military clashes of Black September 1970 in Amman, and to accompany the Palestinian revolution leaders with their forces out of Jordan.

Damascus, we spent about two months with our equipment unopened, until they found us a place and we resumed our work covering the events."[17]

Hind Jawharieh, Hani's Wife Recalls

"During Black September, Hani was filming in Al-Ashrafiyeh, Al-Jofeh and downtown Amman alongside Mustafa. They used to go to Mustafa's home, which he shared with his wife Khadijeh, to rest. Our house burned down, and Hani's passport turned to ashes, so he was unable to join the Palestine Revolution as they left to Lebanon. Hani tried to issue a new passport and was subjected to questioning by the Jordanian Intelligence Service. They asked him for a guarantee of 2000 Jordanian dinars, and of course, we didn't have the money. During this time, he was obliged to open a photography studio with the support of my sister's husband, Michel Sindaha,[18] so that we could survive. Of course, Hani was not satisfied with his work at the studio. His childhood friend Emil Nassar offered him a chance to go photograph in Africa, but he refused. His only concern was to renew his passport so he could rejoin the revolution."[19]

Amneh Naser, Mutee's Wife, Recalls Being Trapped at the Photography Department During the Events of Black September

"During this time, they were all there: Salah, Omar, Mutee', Hani, Mustafa, Naseef, Abu Thareef and Nabil, who lived beside the department in Al-Jofeh. Abu Ammar visited them many times especially during Black September, as he would occasionally spend the night at the photography department.

---

[17] Abu Thareef's memories of the events of Black September were obtained in an interview conducted by the author on August 15, 2016.

[18] Michel Sindaha was a Palestinian militant sentenced to administrative detention on June 9, 1969, by the Israeli Occupation authority because of his syndicate activism. He was exiled to Jordan on April 6, 1970. He became a businessman and a political activist who participated in several committees and organizations and founded several organizations for the protection of Jerusalem and the rights of Jerusalemites.

[19] Hind Jawharieh's memories were obtained in an interview conducted by the author on October 15, 2017.

"After the events of Black September, the photography guys Mutee', Omar, Nabil, Naseef and Abu Thareef moved to Damascus, and they opened a photography department in Al-Mazra'a at the end of 1970. Their space was transformed into an information office, and the photography department moved elsewhere, to Rukn Al-Deen near Abu Jihad's house."[20]

Salah Abu-Hannoud Recounts

"After the Palestinian militants left Jordan at the end of the events at the Jerash Forest,[21] Hani and I remained and were not able to join the revolution's forces, each for a different reason. I remained at Jordan Television after a great deal of effort, connections, and support from the director. I was preparing three programs, but I faced a lot of pressure at work."

Salah recalls Hani's deteriorating economic circumstances when he stayed behind after Black September without any work or income.

> To secure some income for Hani, he and I prepared a film about fine art which was broadcast on Jordanian Television. Then, we started thinking about establishing a photography studio together, however, when Hani's brother-in-law offered to be his partner in the venture, I backed out. I will never forget the extent of Hani's suffering as he worked at the photography studio, away from the revolution. He would constantly say: "After having photographed the fedayeen and the Revolution, I've gone back to shooting birthday parties and weddings." The moment he got a new passport, he decided to join the Revolution in Lebanon at the end of 1975. The year before, in 1974, I found a job in Dubai, which allowed to me to rid myself of the pressure of working for the Jordanian Television after September 1970.[22]

Hind Jawharieh Adds

"I used to go to Lebanon to meet Abu Ammar and Abu Jihad to update them on Hani's news. At the time, we didn't think about money, even

---

[20] Amneh Naser, the wife of Mutee', in an interview conducted by the author on September 24, 2017.

[21] "The Events of Jerash Forest" is the name of the last battle of Black September with severe clashes between the Jordanian Army and the fighters of the Palestinian Revolution (PLO).

[22] Salah Abu Hannoud's memories from an interview conducted by the author on September 25, 2015.

when we were dying of hunger. I recall that when Hani was single, he declined the salary of 15 Jordanian Dinars that he got from Fatah as his brother Riyad had recently graduated from university and was able to work and provide for the family."[23]

Salah Continues

"At the beginning of 1972, I met Mustafa by coincidence in Damascus. I was participating in the Damascus Theatre Festival, and Mustafa was there participating in the Damascus Film Festival for Youth. From him, I learned that the film's name was shortened from *The Armed Revolutionary People Say: No To a Peaceful Solution* to just *No to a Peaceful Solution*. I also learned that the film was attributed to 'Palestine Films' without mentioning or crediting any specific names in that group."[24]

DEPARTURE FROM JORDAN

It was very unfortunate that the founders of the Palestine Film Unit were separated after the events of Black September. Sulafa was still recovering and was partially paralyzed after being shot in the head by accident, so she returned to live with her parents after the revolution's forces left Jordan. Hani was barred from traveling and remained in forced exile.

As for Mustafa, he resigned from the Jordan Television when he learned of a rumor that he was going to be fired despite the fact that he had not yet completed the compulsory work period stipulated by his scholarship. He was supposed to commit to a year and a half of work for every year of education and training he received, and his studies in cinema lasted three years from 1964 to 1967.

BIBLIOGRAPHY

Abu Ghanimeh, Hassan. *Filastin wa-al'Ayn al-Sinima'I [Palestine and the Cinematic Eye]*. Damascus: Ittihad al-Kuttab al-'Arab, 1981.

Abu Ali, Mustafa and Hassan Abu Ghanimeh. *An al-Sinima al-Filastiniyah [About the Palestinian Cinema]*. Beirut: Wihdet Aflam Filastin /Muassaset al-Sinima al-Filastiniyah, 1975.

---

[23] Hind Jawharieh in an interview conducted by the author on October 15, 2017.
[24] Salah Abu Hannoud interview, September 25, 2015.

Chmait, Walid and Guy Hennebelle, eds. *Filastin fi al-Sinima [Palestine in Cinema]*, 2nd ed. Ramallah: Wizarat al-Thaqafah al-Filastiniyah, al-Hay'ah al-'Ammah al-Filastiniyah lil Kitab, 2006.

Al-Najjar, Tayseer. Interview with Mustafa Abu Ali. Source uncertain, possibly *Al Arab Al Yaum* in Jordan, date NA, possibly late 1990s.

CHAPTER 4

The Palestine Film Unit in Lebanon

Mustafa was the only one among the founders of the unit able to join the revolution in Lebanon by the end of 1970, after passing through Damascus and transporting the equipment and filmed material. He knew there were more favorable conditions for making films in Lebanon, and once there, he began working on *With Soul, With Blood*, a film about Black September.

I took a three-week leave from my job to join him and help with his work. Later, in February 1971, I resigned from my job as a clinical psychologist, and left for Beirut to accompany Mustafa and join the revolution.

In his unpublished memoir[1] Mustafa recalls the difficulties he faced in finding a place to work at the Information Office between 1971 and 1972, while he was editing *With Soul, With Blood*, and following its completion.

He recounts: "It is important here to note that these two years, 1971 and 1972, came after the events of Black September in Jordan in 1970, which led to the uprooting of the fedayeen from their main bases in Jordan. The primary task for the Palestinian leadership became finding an alternative base, as well as rebuilding and reorganizing almost everything. In the face of these existential concerns—to be or not to be—cinema seemed to be somewhat of a luxury.

---

[1] Mustafa's memoir discusses the reasons for establishing the Palestinian Cinema Group (PCG) at the end of 1972 and beginning of 1973. He wrote this memoir as he worked on re-establishing the PCG in Ramallah 2004, which was never accomplished.

© The Author(s), under exclusive license to Springer Nature Switzerland AG 2023
K. Habashneh, *Knights of Cinema*, Palgrave Studies in Arab Cinema, https://doi.org/10.1007/978-3-031-18858-9_4

"In characteristic honesty, Kamal Adwan,[2] the martyr and the information representative of Fatah, expressed this sentiment to me in a scene that I remember as if I were reliving it today. We were at the Regional Information Office, the name given to Fatah's information office in Lebanon located in Beirut beside Al-Manara neighborhood at the end of the tram line. It was just before sunset, and I stood on the western balcony of the office as it rained slowly and steadily. Our brother Kamal was with Fawwaz Najiyyeh,[3] who headed the office. I didn't know at the time that they were discussing cinema, but I figured this out later. I suppose the topic had been brought up with Najiyyeh who didn't know what to do about my presence in his office and my desire—or my demand—to use the space for my work after having left Amman. Kamal approached as I stood on the balcony, and said, with sincerity: 'Brother Mustafa, the situation is not suitable for cinema. The conditions are critical. Why don't you try to find work elsewhere?' I was surprised by what I heard, and he left abruptly, avoiding my response to what was just said. I stood there for a second, watching the rain, then climbed down a few steps to find myself walking in the rain, descending from Al-Manara lighthouse towards the beach. I had not come to Beirut looking for work. I had come because of my deep conviction that cinema can serve the cause of the Palestinian people, and I wanted to serve this cause.

"The story with brother Fawwaz Najiyyeh continued as follows: I would frequently go to the Regional Information Office, while trying to find a place for myself and Palestinian cinema.

"I used to stack the few film reels that I had (mostly of Black September) on the table opposite his office. Every time he arrived to find me sitting at my desk across the room, he would alternate his gaze between me and the few film reels, greeting me with a smile before proceeding to enter his office. I noticed this because it occurred repeatedly. Back then, I was working on editing *With Soul, With Blood* at Studio Ba'albak in Beirut. I befriended the head of the studio, Daoud Al-Bina, who was originally Palestinian, and I asked for a few empty boxes, claiming that I had some

---

[2] Kamal Adwan, political and military leader, was one of the founders of Fatah. He was a member of the Central Committee from its inception and served as the head of the information department, then the head of Fatah's work in the Occupied Palestinian Territories. He was assassinated in Beirut in 1973 by the Mossad.

[3] Fawwaz Najiyyeh was head of Fatah's Regional Information Office in Beirut and editor of Fatah's newspaper in English and French.

reels without boxes. He agreed and immediately prepared about 60 large metal boxes for 35 mm reels, which I moved to the Regional Information Office. I chose a time when I was sure Fawwaz wouldn't be there and arranged the boxes so they appeared to be very sizable in number, placing my actual reels on top. I arrived at the office the next day before him, hoping he would be satisfied to greet me with a slight nod and wouldn't enter the room to say hello. I moved towards him and extended one arm to shake his hand, grabbing him and bringing him into the room. Perhaps he was surprised by my behavior, but I did to him what he had done to me, as I kept alternating my gaze, looking at him then back at the reels. He was surprised by the number of boxes in front of him. 'These are all films?' he asked. To prove this, I quickly opened a few of my own boxes that actually contained films, as I memorized their place on top of the empty boxes. I did this until he was convinced that all the boxes were full. When he asked me to stop, I was relieved, because if he hadn't, my plot would have been exposed. After a moment of silence, he then said, 'If this is the situation, then you need an office for yourself,' and he assigned me a room.

"After a while, the Information Office rented an apartment in Al-Nasr building near Al-Kola circle in Beirut in 1972. I had no idea how I got such a relatively large room there. It was called the Palestine Film office.

"Our brother Kamal Adwan was [as mentioned] the head of Fatah's Information Office and his deputy was Majed Abu Sharar.[4] I can't quite remember whether this happened before or after the Damascus film festival where we won the documentary prize for *With Soul, With Blood*. If it was after the festival, as it likely was, no doubt this prize helped us get a large room. But the prize's effect did not last very long. After a short while, as I was going from the Palestine Film office to the adjacent room, I overheard Majed on the phone with the Fatah office in Algeria. With his back turned to me, I heard him ask the person on the other line if they could find me a job in Algerian cinema. I became angry because I had not asked anyone to find me another job. I quickly remembered the words of our brother Kamal on the balcony of the old office on that rainy day. When he realized that I had overheard the conversation and was angry, Majed tried to ease the situation. I found myself saying, 'You want to send

---

[4] Majed Abu-Sharar was the head of Information at Fatah, and then the head of the Unified Information. He was elected to the Central Committee of Fatah in the fourth conference in 1980 and became the head of the Fatah organization of the Occupied Palestinian Territories. He was assassinated by the Israeli Mossad in Rome in 1981.

me to Algeria. Why don't you just go there yourself? I am staying here, brother Majed. And just so you know, this is the Palestinian people's revolution.' However, after I had calmed down, I realized that the issue was not personal, and perhaps the presence of the cinema activities was a burden on the office, whether on its financing, or through claiming a large room in the limited apartment space with no more than three or four rooms. Whatever the situation and its justifications, I found myself to be an unbearable guest of the Information Office. I alternated between being sympathetic and feeling upset. I would sometimes tell myself 'If this office doesn't want cinema, then they can go to hell, and I can work independently.' And the situation kept weighing on me until I came up with the idea of the Palestinian Cinema Group, and I started communicating with people to realize it."

The establishment of the Palestinian Cinema Group has its own story, which will be told later.

WITH SOUL, WITH BLOOD

Since the early days of conceptualizing establishing the Palestine Film Unit at the end of 1968, the three filmmakers realized that they were confronting a different type of cinema from what was known. Some of the questions that they asked themselves were described by Mustafa Abu Ali in his article "The Establishment of Palestinian Cinema and Its Directions":[5]

> Since the beginning, we thought and wondered whether the artistic and aesthetic values that we had studied fit our audience. Do we address our audience using the same tools we had learned in London and Cairo? Or do we develop a new, different, and special approach? Can we express the experiences of the Palestinian Revolution with traditional tools outside of revolutionary conditions? Will we imitate these methods and art forms innovated and used by cinema tied to the colonial experience? Or will we develop methods and a cinematic language specific to us, with links to our Arab culture and the specificity of the Palestinian Revolution and its conditions? These are the questions that shaped the work and direction of the Palestine Film Unit. We realized, at the time, when we posed this question, that a

[5] This article, co-authored by Mustafa Abu Ali and Hassan Abu Ghanimeh, was republished in the Arabic edition of the book *Palestine in Cinema* (Ramallah: Palestinian Ministry of Culture, 2006), p 26–27, 1977.

long and difficult journey lies ahead of us. We needed to develop a cinema specific to our people, to express our peoples' war, and the film *With Soul, With Blood* can be considered an index for the style and approach of the Palestine Film Unit.

In His Book *About the Palestinian Cinema* Co-authored with Hassan Abu Ghanimeh, Mustafa Described the Challenges Following Black September

After the events of Black September, and the revolution's evacuation from Jordan, the unit's work was confined, unfortunately, to a single effort from among the three founders of the Palestine Film Unit. With the absence of the founding photographers Sulafa and Hani, I was forced to carry all the responsibility myself.

During this period, I considered making a film about the events of Black September because a lot of people and politicians were discussing it. After long and serious conversations, I was convinced of the need to offer a holistic political analysis of what transpired. With this, the main imperative became sketching out the political analysis that formed the basis of the film. In other words, I chose the approach of militant cinema instead of documentary film, as political analysis came to replace the traditional scenario. The political elite and leaders of the revolution helped to develop the political analysis and the artistic team (comprised of myself) translated the analysis cinematically. The material filmed during Black September was used alongside additional footage captured during national and cultural events, or coverage of political and military activities.

The discussions and debates amongst the political cadres and the artistic team continued throughout the editing period which lasted more than four months, as several tests for the style and pacing of the film were conducted. One example was experimentation on the first segment which used animated cartoons to clarify the content. A number of tests on the rhythm of the drawings and images segment were shown to audiences at the camp, and after soliciting feedback, the rhythm was determined to be too fast. The segment was replaced with a theatrical sequence performed by children.

When *With Soul, With Blood* premiered at the First International Film Festival for Youth in Damascus in April 1972, I remember that it sparked a wide debate about alternative documentary techniques that were different from what was known of the documentary film tradition. Mustafa discussed this with other filmmakers, as he identified himself as the director of the film. This was not clear to everyone, because the film was credited to the Palestine Film Unit. He also discussed the Palestine Film Unit's vision of its role in a revolutionary cinema.

In this festival, *With Soul, With Blood* received the prize in the mid-length documentary film category. In my meeting with the novelist Rashad Abu Shawer,[6] who had participated in the festival, I was reminded of something Mustafa had said that represented the unit's revolutionary cinema: "We are revolutionary filmmakers releasing twenty-four images every second," which was received by a hurricane of applause and admiration from the audience.

During the festival, we met several filmmakers and critics. Among them, I remember the well-known Egyptian critic Samir Farid, Egyptian director Salah Al-Tahumi, Lebanese critics Walid Chmait and Samir Nasri, and a number of Syrian filmmakers, among whom I remember Nabil Al-Maleh. Among the Iraqi filmmakers I remember Faysal Al-Yasiri and Abdelhadi Al-Rawi, and from Kuwait the director Khaled Al-Sedeeq, whose film *Bas Ya Bahar* was the first Kuwaiti film to gain recognition from critics and the jury, winning the best narrative film prize. This opened the horizon for Mustafa and the newly established unit to build relationships and connections. We met the young Jordanian journalist Hassan Abu Ghanimeh, who was particularly impressed by *With Soul, With Blood* and expressed his interest in working part-time with the Palestine Film Unit, though he was constantly traveling between Beirut and Damascus for his journalism work.

Hassan Abu Ghanimeh

Hassan Abu Ghanimeh was born in the Jordanian city of Irbid in 1948. He completed his primary and secondary education at Al-'Uroubah School in Irbid, a private school owned by his father.

His sister Sahar, who is a few years younger, recalls:

He received a scholarship to study medicine in Romania through his uncle who was the Jordanian ambassador to Syria. After completing a year in the

---

[6] Rashad Abu Shawer, a Palestinian writer and novelist, participated in The International Film Festival for Youth in Damascus. He wrote the novel *Days of Love and Death* which Mustafa later adapted into a screenplay for a feature narrative film.

faculty of medicine, he switched to film directing. After that, he was forced to return to Jordan because of a health condition, and his family didn't allow him to return to Romania. He enjoyed reading and journalistic writing, and he spent all of his income on watching films at the cinema. When he was a teenager, he used to create for his younger siblings a newspaper that detailed the events of his life and the films he'd seen. He also tried to make films using what resembles a wonder box for his siblings, friends and neighbors.[7]

Hassan started preparing some writings and publications with Mustafa about the work of the Palestine Film Unit and participated in the unit's delegations to Arab and international festivals. Because of this, he witnessed an important period of the development of the unit between 1972 and the end of 1975 and was among the first to document Palestinian cinema of the revolution in his book *Palestine and the Cinematic Eye* in 1981.

Building Audience Engagement

One of the important field experiences undertaken by the Palestine Film Unit was the public questionnaire related to the films it produced, including *With Soul, With Blood*, and to the films collected from allied revolutionary movements.[8] The unit would prepare a series of printed questions that would be distributed to the audience before the screening, to be completed after watching the film. Many people filled them out, and their responses allowed us to conclude the following:

- There was a wide reception to viewing the Palestinian films, because people were seeing themselves, their children, and the fighters, on screen through these films for the first time.
- The films of the popular revolutions from places like Vietnam, Cuba, and Algeria were well received alongside Palestinian films.
- The audiences preferred a realistic style to a symbolic style.
- Some of the audience members who were accustomed to watching commercial cinema would feel upset or surprised at the beginning, but after discussing the films, especially *With Soul, With Blood*, they would express interest in watching the films a second time.

[7] Sahar Abu Ghanimeh interview conducted by the author on October 17, 2017.
[8] Mustafa Abu Ali and Hassan Abu Ghanimeh, *About the Palestinian Cinema* (Beirut: Palestine Film Unit, 1975), p. 26–27.

Between 1971 and 1972, Mustafa worked mostly alone and had to film while supervising the audio recording. I had to occasionally help with whatever he needed.

I recall having to photograph or record sounds at protests and celebrations with his guidance. I remember the difficulties I faced working with the Nagra recorder because it was heavy and very sophisticated. In 1972 Mustafa worked almost singlehandedly in filming, directing, and producing two films: *Al-Arqoub* and *Zionist Aggression*. He also applied for grants from Arab Cinema institutes for developing filmmaking skills to compensate for the absences of Sulafa and Hani. Below are excerpts of some memories from and about the few people who worked with the photography department in Damascus in the early 1970s.

Recollections of PFU Training

Naseef, the Photographer, Recalls His Time with the Photography Department in Damascus
"At the beginning of 1972, Nabil and I went to Baghdad for a film training workshop. Mutee' and Omar also attended the same training in 1973."[9]

Abu Thareef recalls
"Nabil and Naseef attended a short workshop in Baghdad. Later, Omar and Mutee' attended a filmmaking workshop in Baghdad in 1972–1973. I attended a filmmaking workshop in Hungary in 1975."[10]
The photography guys in Damascus also came to Beirut occasionally to cover important events or celebrations.

Amneh Naser recalls husband Mutee
After the workshop [in Baghdad], in 1973, Omar returned to Beirut, as Mutee' went back to join Nabil and Naseef at the photography department in Damascus."[11]

Amneh Naser remembers that they filmed the events of the October 1973 war in the areas of Beqa'a, Aintoura, and Jabal Al-Sheikh. "Mutee' worked as the head of the photography department in Damascus until the end of 1975, when he moved to work at the Palestine Film Unit that developed into the Palestinian Cinema Institution in Beirut" (Fig. 4.1).

---

[9] From Naseef's interview with the author conducted on June 27, 2014.
[10] From Abu Thareef's interview with the author conducted on August 15, 2016.
[11] From Amneh Naser's interview with the author conducted on September 24, 2017.

Fig. 4.1   Photographer Mutee' at Jabal Al-Shaikh, October, 1973

Nabil's Participation in Military Operations[12]

In an interview I conducted with Nabil Mahdi in 2017, he told me about his experiences as a photographer participating in military operations. "In mid-1969, the revolution conducted an important military operation in the area of Al-Himmeh, resulting in clashes extending around 40 kilometres. Hani was among the fighters as he photographed the operation."

Nabil continued: "When we accompanied the fighters on operations, the command to fire came from the photographer, after the camera was set up. This is what I experienced when I joined the fighters in Fatah's operation in Al-Khalsa,[13] and when I covered the shelling on Kafrchouba and Kafrhamam at the beginning of the seventies."

Nabil also remembered an incident where the Lebanese newspaper *Al-Muharir* had to publish photos of the battles at Al-Khalsa and Qiryat Shmona on its front page.

He described the story of photographing the shelling of Al-Khalsa settlement:

> I accompanied an operation conducted by Fatah fighters at the beginning of the 1970's. After the shelling, I encountered a journalist working for *Al-Muharir* newspaper. He was disappointed for failing to photograph the operation and asked me to share some photographs with him. I shared my photos with him on the condition that they be published on the newspaper's front page.
>
> Sure enough, the photo appeared the next morning on the front page. Upon seeing it, the head of Fatah's information office, Majed Abu Sharar, angrily summoned me to answer how *Al-Muharir's* photographer had documented the event. After explaining what had happened with the photographer, Majed understood the truth of the situation and got up to kiss me on the forehead.[14]

Nabil continued his work with the photography department after the workshop in Baghdad. His primary job, however, was to partake in military operations in the West Bank.

---

[12] From Nabil Mahdi's interview with the author conducted on September 27, 2017.

[13] Al-Khalsa operation was undertaken by Fatah at the beginning of 1971. During the operation, fighters made their way to the north of Occupied Palestine, where they launched rockets into the village of Al-Khalsa. It is different from the 1974 Al-Khalsa operation undertaken by fighters of the General Command of the Popular Front for the Liberation of Palestine.

[14] At the time *Al Muharir* and Arabic newspapers did not publish photographs of Fatah fighter operations. Only Fatah published photos of its operations in its newspaper.

Nabil and Naseef continued their work in the photography department in Damascus, after completing their training in Bagdad at the end of 1972. They used to cover the revolutionary activities in Syria and occasionally military operations. Around the middle of 1975, the Palestinian revolutionary activities encountered some difficulties from the Syrian regime. At that time Mutee had been asked to join the PCI in Beirut, while Naseef and Nabil were obliged to withdraw from the PFU or PCI to return to Jordan for personal reasons, and they could not return to Syria. Later Naseef opened a photography studio in Al-Wihdat camp, and Nabil opened one in the neighborhood of Al-Rusaifa, near Amman.[15]

DIFFERENCES BETWEEN CINEMA AND JOURNALISM

After the Israeli air raids on Al-Arqoub in Southern Lebanon in 1972, the Palestine Film Unit produced a film entitled *Al-Arqoub*. After screening the first cut of the film to the political and information cadres within Fatah, the conversation between the filmmakers and the journalists began to reveal to Mustafa a disagreement over the concept of cinema and cinematic film. The journalists, supported by the political cadres, disagreed with some of the artistic language of the film. Some contentious aspects included the fade-out of an anthem in the background of a scene, the incorporation of only small segments of statements or interviews with leaders, or using a chorus to narrate the commentary, among other details recounted by Hassan Abu Ghanimeh and Mustafa.[16]

About this Abu Ghanimeh said: "Mustafa was not able to convey the message of his film because he did not reach the battlefield with his camera early enough, as he had when he filmed *With Soul, With Blood,* and his film relies on shots filmed during other battles."

At the same time, Mustafa noted, as Ghanimeh quotes:

This film is about a battle that took place between the Fedayeen and the Zionist forces in Southern Lebanon in 1972. However, fifteen minutes of the very valuable material we shot was damaged when it was developed. What remained were scenes of raids on Rashaya. In this film, I intended on using a group to read the voiceover; in other words, the film was narrated collectively. Though the execution of the idea was not as good as it could have been, I reserve the right to continue to experiment with this idea in future with the aim of breaking from individuality and encouraging a feeling of collectivity.

[15] From Naseef's interview conducted by the author on June 27, 2014.
[16] Hassan Abu Ghanimeh, *Palestine and the Cinematic Eye* (Damascus: Union of Arab Writers, 1981), p 283–284.

The disagreement reached the extent where the leadership (of the Information Office) demanded that work on the film should stop, and it should not be sent to participate in the second Damascus Film Festival. This compelled me to personally smuggle the film to participate in the festival, but unfortunately *Al-Arqoub* was not distributed or screened. This is where the filmmakers realized the extent of the difference between their perspective and that of the information and political leaders on cinema.

THE PALESTINE FILM UNIT'S CINEMATIC EXPERIENCE

The experience of *With Soul, With Blood* and the review of the literature on Palestinian cinema[17] reveal that Palestinian revolutionary filmmaking was inspired in its principles, aims, and methods by the popular revolutions in Vietnam, Cuba, and Algeria. Cinema is, by nature, a popular and all-encompassing art that is able to innovate simple and beautiful ways to communicate dynamically with the people. Revolutionary cinema actively looked for a unique language and cinematic aesthetic that is simple, clear, and easily felt by the masses. It captures the reality lived by the popular audiences in all of its facets and conveys a message while simultaneously serving the peoples' interests by appealing to their morale and spirit. Revolutionary cinema helps the people understand their problems and realities by exposing the tactics of colonization and political, military, and cultural occupation. It allows the people to create solutions to confront this reality while encouraging them to continue their struggle. As such, filmmakers had to remain close to the popular audiences, to understand their needs and experiences. The film unit decided to avoid using two languages: one for the people, and one for the world. They believed that what expresses the peoples' desires can communicate their cause to the world. They also decided to follow a participatory approach by engaging all members of the unit in the work, departing from rigidly defined roles, and adopting instead a fluid approach that involved everyone in all stages, from the idea to the scenario to the filming and audio recording, and so on.

This precaution underlined the Palestine Film Unit's understanding of the revolution's context of crisis and battles where the team could lose one of its members at any moment.

The militant experience was exceptional because it strayed away from typical Arab cinema which was influenced by Hollywood, turning to

---

[17] Abu Ali and Abu Ghanimeh, *About the Palestinian Cinema*, 1975, p. 27–30.

methods inspired by the struggle and its peoples' culture. The unit was innovative, but it stayed true to the people's cause. Their work was collaborative to the extent that the early films produced in the first years did not bear the name of a specific director and artistic team, but rather the name "Palestine Films" instead. These militant filmmakers are distinguished for the dedication they poured into their work, and the courage they exhibited in the face of danger. This was expressed in the Palestine Film Unit's first statement issued in April 1972, during the Damascus Festival for Youth Cinema.[18]

The Experience of the Film Zionist Aggression

In this film, Mustafa offered another expression of his vision for militant cinema, as he filmed everything and left the shots as they were, unedited. The film begins with the sound of Israeli military planes, then it presents a title slide in Arabic, followed by an English and French translation to indicate the date and place of the air raids. The film proceeds to display, silently, the tragic and barbaric results of the air raids. Here, Mustafa did not want to sugarcoat death, as he would say, choosing instead to show raw shots, occasionally overlaid with soft music. Then, he shifted to images of the popular protests that condemned the aggression and called for steadfastness and resistance, followed by sounds of counter-missiles, which he considered to be the decisive response of the Palestinian Revolution.

When *Zionist Aggression* was screened at the Third World Cinema Committee meeting in Algeria in 1973, the Cuban director Santiago Álvarez,[19] who was among the most prominent third world militant cinema directors, addressed Mustafa saying:

> Your screening of Palestinian cinema has contributed greatly to informing us about the Palestinian Revolution and its history. We used to hear a lot about the Palestinian Revolution, but watching your films has developed our understanding, as we learned precisely about the size of the revolution and its history of struggle. We are pleased to know that there are filmmakers among you who fully understand the power of this art as a weapon in the revolution's arsenal, and it has already been deployed seriously and with great command.

---

[18] "Palestine Film Manifesto" is at the end of the book, Appendix A.

[19] Santiago Álvarez, is considered the father of militant cinema in Cuba and one of the symbols of militant cinema globally.

Both *Zionist Aggression* and *With Soul, With Blood* were screened at this forum (Abu Ghanimeh 1981).

Alvarez added: "I consider the film *Zionist Aggression* to be one of the most important and unique documents that highlights the savagery of Zionist aggression and renders visible its crimes through a raw documentary approach that dispels any doubt. It is one of the most important films I've seen that relies exclusively on raw footage, which in its most truthful form strengthens and multiplies its influence."[20]

I learned from Mustafa upon his return from the meeting that he was pleased with the outcome, especially with the recognition he received from Santiago Álvarez who gave him the nickname "Young Álvarez" and remarked, "You are the first cinema unit to join an armed resistance movement from its inception."

Journalist and militant writer Nazeh Abu Nidal[21] recalls:

I personally criticized Mustafa's decision to incorporate a mutilated head and the extended shots of children's corpses in *Zionist Aggression*. It is borrowed from traditional cinema in that such sadistic shots provoke discomfort in the viewer. I was surprised when Mustafa returned from one of the festivals and told me. "The shots you did not like, Abu Nidal, shocked the audience and the critics. It was the shock I wanted to provoke." The film won the praise of the jury and received a prize.[22]

The film also won the symposium prize at the Karlovy Vary Film Festival in 1974.

MILITANT CINEMA RELATIONS: THE PALESTINE FILM UNIT AND THIRD WORLD CINEMA

A group of Argentinian filmmakers arrived in Beirut in 1971. I remember this clearly as we hosted them at our first house after fleeing Jordan, the house in Burj Abu-Haydar. The group was comprised of three people: two men and a woman. I will never forget the two men's names, as they were

---

[20] Abu Ghanimeh, *Palestine and the Cinematic Eye*, p. 286.

[21] Nazeh Abu Nidal (real name: Ghattas Swais), a militant in the Fateh movement, a journalist, and political delegate among the militants. He came from a Jordanian family from the town of Al-Fuhais.

[22] Interview with Nazeh Abu Nidal about his experience with the Palestine Film Unit, November 15, 2018.

both called Jorge (George), and we would call them Jorge One and Jorge Two. They came to learn about the Palestinian Revolution up close, to make a film about it. I learned the full name of one of the directors, Jorge Denti, when we heard that he is the director of the film *Palestine, Another Vietnam*.

While conducting the research for this book, I discovered the name of the second Jorge, Jorge Giannoni, and the woman who accompanied them, Manuela Generali, who was Jorge Denti's Swiss girlfriend. And I remembered our discussions on the Palestinian cause and women's role in the revolution.

The group would sometimes bring back food, perhaps so that they wouldn't burden me. I also recall that they ate a lot of yoghurt, maybe because they were on tight budget.

In his book about Palestine and Montoneros, *Montoneros Y Palestina*,[23] Pablo Robledo[24] discusses the relationship between the Palestine Liberation Organization and the Montoneros, an Argentinian militant movement. He saw these two organizations as, "at a certain time in the seventies, the biggest and most important revolutions globally in terms of power and organization. There was solidarity and cooperation amongst them in various ways and in different places."

In the fifth chapter of the book Robledo explores the relationship between Argentinian Third World Cinema and Palestinian cinema. He describes the experiences of Jorge Denti, his Swiss partner Manuela Generali, and Jorge Giannoni in their movements between Lebanon, Jordan, and Syria in 1971 while filming *Palestine, Another Vietnam*:

> At their arrival, Denti, Giannoni and Manuela are received by Fatah cadres, with whom they made their first contacts. They would be the persons in charge to offer the necessary access to filming and provide them with a

---

[23] *Montoneros Y Palestina: Dela Revolution a La Dictadura* by Pablo Robledo, Editorial Planeta, Buenos Aires, Argentina, 2018, chapter five. In general, the book discusses the relationship between the Palestine Liberation Organization and the Argentinian Montoneros movement between 1970 and 1982.

[24] Pablo Robledo, an Argentinian critic and filmmaker, specialized in political studies and international relations. He worked as a journalist, documentary filmmaker, and historian in the last thirty-three years of his life. His writings are about the relationship between revolutions and liberation movements around the world and their cultural expression in the 1970s, including Third World Cinema and cinema from the Palestinian Revolution.

certain security. The massive arrival of the Palestinian cadres to the city in 1971 was very recent and the construction of the powerful political-military apparatus which they would arrange in the future was still emerging. Furthermore, they [the filmmakers] maintained other contacts and filmed with units of the Popular Front (PFLP) and the Democratic Front of the Liberation of Palestine (DFLP) apart from off-screen Palestinian politicians, Lebanese militants and social leaders inside the refugee camps.

Robledo describes the filmmakers' limited budget, which confined them to sleeping in their Kombi mini-van and eating very little, because they were committed to filming the revolution. He mentions how a new world slowly opened up to them through their visits to refugee camps, military training bases, hospitals and social centers, poor neighborhoods, and political meeting stages. Manuela's presence was critical to entering women's spaces.

> The fact that Manuela was part of the team gave them access to places and situations that would have been inaccessible otherwise: delivery rooms for Palestinian women, field hospitals and bases, hospitalization areas for the injured in combat. The presence of a woman broke the ice easily and guaranteed the availability of witnesses and unique images.

Robledo also describes the help they received from Palestinian filmmakers and intellectuals: "Meanwhile intellectual Palestinians and filmmakers based in Beirut provided them with archival material concerning the resistance that would be of an inestimable value during the editing."

To finish the film, they headed to Rome, where they received funding from Enzo Rossellini,[25] who upon viewing their footage offered to produce the film and gave them a Moviola to edit it.

Robledo mentions the success of the completed film in Baghdad:

> Its directors, attracted by the return of democracy and the revolutionary spirit, returned to Argentina in 1973, the year in which Mustafa Abu Ali contacted Denti and Giannoni to screen the film *Palestine, another Vietnam* in the Cinema and Television Festival that took place in Bagdad from March 19 to 22. In the category dedicated to Palestine, Argentina won the Jury Special Prize for the best film.

---

[25] Enzo Rossellini, son of the famous Italian director Roberto Rossellini, worked as a cinema producer.

According to Robledo, Denti greatly admired Mustafa for making history and putting Palestinian revolutionary cinema on the map, particularly in transforming Golda Meir's infamous reference to Palestinians ("they do not exist") into a film.

After facing a lot of political difficulties, the Argentinian filmmakers (including Denti and Giannoni) were able to establish a collective for Third World Cinema which met in Algeria that same year in 1973 (Fig. 4.2). Mustafa Abu Ali, Hassan Abu Ghanimeh, and Ibrahim Naser attended the meeting.

Expansion of Film Production in the PLO[26]

The beginning and middle of the 1970s witnessed an expansion of the circle of filmmaking across several PLO political organizations, departments, and institutes that produced various films alongside the Palestine Film Unit/Palestinian Cinema Institution. They are described below.

Fig. 4.2 Credit frame from *Palestine, Another Vietnam* by the Argentinian Collectivo C3M, Cinema del Terzo Mondo

---

[26] A list of Palestinian films produced by the organizations and committees working in cinema in the PLO can be found in Appendix C.

The Department of Culture and Information (Palestine Liberation Organization)

Hussein Oudat's book *Cinema and the Palestinian Cause* offers a very accurate account of the development of the many film groups that were allied with the Palestinian Revolution. Here he describes the Department of Culture and Arts:[27]

> The Department of Culture and Information was established in 1965, and its name was later changed to the Department of Culture and Arts. Its aims, according to the Palestinian fine artist Ismael Shammout, were to provide people with the desired information through artistic tools, exhibitions, posters, photographs, dramatic arts and cinema. The department held various exhibitions and developed a photographic archive. The photography unit was established in 1967 and filmmaking began using an 8mm camera.

In 1973, the Department of Culture and Arts, under the leadership of the politician Abdallah Hourani,[28] took over the task of film production. It produced its first film in 1972 entitled *Youth Camps*, directed by the artist Ismael Shammout. By the end of the 1980s, the department had produced twenty documentary films and three television series

Committee of Central Information/Arts Section/the Popular Front for the Liberation of Palestine

This is also from Oudat's book:[29]

> The Committee in the Popular Front for the Liberation of Palestine was established in 1970. It was initially interested in theatre, but then formed a cinema unit and released a statement expressing its understanding of the work of Palestinian cinema. It declared: "After the establishment of cinema supporting the Palestinian resistance struggle, the reality of the revolution has been recorded. In its beginnings it (the cinema unit of the arts department) did not go beyond recording documents, without expanding in vision or implementation." The statement also indicated the need to make Palestinian films public, and to preserve film and photographic documents

---

[27] Husain Oudat. *Cinema, and the Palestinian Cause* (Damascus: Dar Al-Ahli, 1987), p 65.

[28] Abdallah Hourani, Palestinian militant and intellectual, was head of the Department of Culture of the PLO since 1974. He was elected as a member of the executive committee of the PLO in the Palestine National Council in 1984.

[29] Oudat, *Cinema, and the Palestinian Cause*, 1987, p 65.

of the Palestinian Revolution in a specialized archive that will serve as a reference and material to train militants in filmmaking.

The Committee produced its first film, *On the Road to the Palestinian Revolution*, directed by Fouad Zantout in 1971.[30] By 1982, it had produced nine documentary films, one fiction film *Return to Haifa* directed by Qasem Hawal,[31] and one news reel.

Artistic Committee/the Democratic Front for the Liberation of Palestine

Hassan Abu Ghanimeh describes the Artistic Committee in *Palestine and the Cinematic Eye*:[32]

The committee produced its first film in 1973, as it joined several political and cultural elite, but lacked specialized filmmakers, with the exception of the director, cinematographer and editor Rafiq Hajjar,[33] who played the largest role in the committee's success. The committee did not have full equipment or specialized technicians, and it often relied on equipment and experts from studios in Beirut to produce its work.

The first film that the committee made of the eight films it produced by the 1980s was *Al-Tareeq*.

The Palestine Film Unit's Expanded Relations

The PFU participated in a number of international festivals including the Damascus International Film Festival for Youth, Leipzig Festival, Oberhausen Film Festival in Germany, Algeria Festival, the Baghdad

---

[30] Fouad Zantout, a Lebanese filmmaker and editor, directed films produced by the PFLP including *On the Road to the Palestinian Revolution* (1970), *Black Papers* (1979), *The News Reel, First Edition* (1979), and *Betrayal* (1980).

[31] Qasem Hawal, Iraqi theatre and film director, joined the PFLP in 1970, and directed several documentary films for them including *Alnnahr Al-Bared* in (1971, *The Guns Will Not Be Silent* (1973), *Our Small Houses* (1974), *Return to Haifa* (1982), and *Sabra and Shatila* (1983).

[32] Abu Ghanimeh, *Palestine and the Cinematic Eye*, p. 315–320.

[33] Rafiq Hajjar, a Lebanese director, cinematographer, and film editor, was a militant who joined the ranks of the Democratic Front for the Liberation of Palestine (DFLP), where he directed most of their films, including *Al-Tareeq* (1972), *The United Guns* (1973), *Palestinian May* (1974), and *The Intifada* (1975).

International Festival for Palestinian Films and TV Programs, the Karlovy
Vary Film Festival, and others I don't remember. The unit received many
prizes, and its network began to expand as they received training grants for
the unit's younger members through relationships with film festival directors and other cinema initiatives. It received grants for photojournalism
training, and for cinema training.

The unit later received several scholarships from the German Democratic
Republic and the Soviet Union. It also received equipment donated from
several countries including the Soviet Union, Libya, and others. The
equipment included an editing machine called a Moviola that I later used
to view and sort film footage dating back to 1968.

Hassan Abu Ghanimeh

"From the beginning of 1972 until the end of 1975, the Palestine Film
Unit got the chance to learn about radical and militant cinema experiences
through international film festivals and conferences. They learned specifically from the experiences of Vietnam, Cuba, Algeria, and the Soviet
Union, in addition to the experiences of radical and militant filmmakers
from Latin America, Europe, North America, Africa and Asia. Exposure to
the opinions of filmmakers including the Cuban Santiago Álvarez, German
Manfred Foss, French Serge Le Peron, Indian Mrinal Sen, and Senegalese
Ousmane Sembène, among others, convinced us that the unit was headed
in the right direction alongside other militant and revolutionary cinemas."[34]

The Palestine Film Unit played an important role in presenting the
cause of the Palestinian people, and highlighting its struggle against
Zionist occupation, in the hopes of achieving its national goals of liberation and independence.

Palestinian films became very popular at festivals, winning prizes in
Damascus, Carthage, Karlovy Vary, Leipzig, Berlin, Moscow, and other
places. As a result, Palestinian cinema started to eclipse Israeli cinema at
international festivals, as expressed by a cartoon published in the Israeli
newspaper *Haaretz*, supplied to us by the Hebrew department of the
Palestine Research Center. I distinctly remember this cartoon. It became

---

[34] Abu Ali and Abu Ghanimeh, *About the Palestinian Cinema*, 1975, p. 28.

part of the photographic archive of the Palestinian Cinema Institution, which is currently held in an unknown place.

In the period between 1971 and 1974, I was not working full-time with the PFU, but rather in a parallel Fatah political organization and with the preparatory committee for the Palestinian Women's Union in Lebanon. The head of the Department of Popular Mobilization for the PLO made me head of the membership committee that was responsible for recruiting members in preparation for the first union conference to be held in Lebanon. In addition, I was responsible for re-structuring the committees of the Palestinian Women's Union in the camps. We organized the first conference for the Palestinian Women's Union in May 1972, in the Dbayeh Camp of Lebanon.

Fatah's Women's Office in Lebanon was established, and I worked there alongside the militant leader Abu Omar,[35] Jehan Helou,[36] and others to oversee and follow up on women's work in political mobilization and the Union of Palestinian Women. I also started working as a psychologist at the Martyr's Children School at the village of Souq Al Gharb in the mountains of Lebanon in 1973.

At the same time, I helped Mustafa with specific tasks once he began working on *With Soul, With Blood* alone. I remember, for example, purchasing black fabric and planning the darkroom where film was developed and printed. I would also look for the required film material (film shots, reels, video tapes) and would occasionally record sound with him, in addition to taking pictures when the photographers who usually came from Damascus to cover important events were unavailable.

In addition, I accompanied some of the Arab and foreign filmmakers throughout the production process and sometimes I would help recruit extras for films. For example, when we worked with the Algerian director Mohammad Saleem Riyad who made *We Will Return* in 1971–1972, I served as production assistant with Mr. Mustafa Belleil. I also helped with

---

[35] Abu Omar (real name: Hanna Mikhail), a militant leader and thinker, joined Fatah in 1968, after leaving his position as a professor at Georgetown University. He worked on political mobilization at the fighter bases. He was among the most prolific and progressive leaders of Fatah. Later he disappeared with a group of political elites who were aboard a boat headed toward Tripoli in Northern Lebanon in 1976.

[36] Jehan Helou was a militant, researcher at the Palestine Studies Institute, member of the Women's Office, and wife of Abu Omar.

scheduling meetings with the political cadres, revolutionary leadership, and Palestinian families, where I sometimes provided translation, as I did with the Danish director Nils Vest when he shot *Oppressed People Are Always Right* in 1973.

FILM SCREENINGS AND DISTRIBUTION

The experience of film screenings played a major role in the establishment and development of the work of the Palestine Film Unit.

Mustafa Abu Ali explained how critical this was:[37]

> The work of militant cinema cannot be complete without screening the films to audiences participating in the revolution. The filmmaker must attend these screenings to the people, and this can be announced or discreet depending on what fits the revolutionary moment.

Mustafa added in another context, "We, the Palestine Film Unit, consider screening our films as complementary to our production work. We express the spirit and struggle of our people, so we must understand the reactions of our people to these films, and oftentimes, conversations and discussions arise, that I must admit are very useful to me."

I elaborated on this in the following excerpts from an article I wrote under the name Khadijah Abu Ali, entitled "Film Screenings and their Beginnings":[38]

> From the onset of the Palestine Film Unit's work, there were two 16 mm projectors and a number of militant films that were presented as a gift to the Palestinian revolution. The early beginning of the unit's cinematic work was carrying these films around and screening them at the fedayeen bases in the Jordan Valley. These screenings were met with great enthusiasm, as they presented a chance to share with our militants and audiences the experiences of other peoples and their struggles. During this period, the screenings served exclusively as tools of political education. They instilled in the group a conviction about the role of cinema in political education.

---

[37] Abu Ali and Abu Ghanimeh, *About Palestinian Cinema*, 1975, p. 31

[38] Khadijeh Abu Ali (the name I used in the Palestinian cultural circles given my work with my husband, Mustafa Abu Ali), "Film Screenings and Their Beginnings," *Palestinian Image*, Second issue, March (Beirut: Palestinian Cinema Institution, 1979), p. 31.

The film screenings developed after the unit completed its first film *No to a Peaceful Solution*, which expressed the people's popular rejection of the Rogers Plan.

My article discusses the experience of screening the first film to militants and audiences who saw themselves, for the first time, replacing film celebrities they had traditionally seen in cinemas. The PFU wanted to hear their thoughts and reactions to the film. They learned a lot from the experience of that first film which they themselves criticized for its weak points, despite popular reception from the militants and the people. The unit's experience of this first film informed their second film, *With Soul, With Blood*.

During the early days in Lebanon, Mustafa and I resumed the screenings while he worked on *With Soul, With Blood*. He would organize screenings for the fighters at the bases, while I organized screenings in the refugee camps, where I spent a lot of time through my work with the Palestinian Women's Union.

In my article I describe places where the films were shown, documenting how the screenings were initially organized by members of the unit who trained volunteers from the student union to meet the increasing demand for film screenings. They set up events at schools, universities, clubs, refugee camps, and popular areas. The political mobilization department also trained its personnel to screen films on the military bases. After that, in 1971, voluntary teams were established to organize screenings.

The unit was in the early stages of testing its ideas about revolutionary cinema and sought to experiment with its questionnaire strategy. So, we drafted a number of questions that were distributed to the audience before the screening to solicit their opinions on films. Around the mid-1970s, a department for popular information was established under the Unified Information Office, and the film screenings fell under its scope of work. This department was responsible for screening films in conferences, festivals, and during important national celebrations.

My article also highlights the circulation of the films of the Palestine Film Unit/Palestinian Cinema Institution[39] abroad in international film festivals, through programs and offices of the PLO, the activities of the Palestinian student unions in various countries, as well as Palestine Solidarity committees and groups across the world.

---

[39] The Palestine Film Unit (PFU) would later reformulate into the short-lived Palestine Cinema Group (PCG) in 1973 and then the Palestinian Cinema Institution in 1974/1975.

Connected to this distribution was the cinema library, or cinematheque, that was created by the PFU/PCI. It was comprised of Palestinian films and progressive and militant films from other global revolutionary movements. These films were later shown in the screening room located in the basement of the Unified Information building, where the offices of the PCI and the Palestine News Agency (also called Wafa) were located.

As for film distribution, the PFU/PCI would distribute its completed films to the PLO office, to be screened through their programs and the programs of the different branches of the Palestinian Student Union. Some festivals would also hold onto copies of the films they screened through their programs. This was the case especially in festivals around the Arab world, including Damascus, Baghdad, Cairo, Algeria, Tunis, and Morocco. I don't know whether these festivals bought copies of these films. Frankly, most of the films were distributed to raise awareness about the Palestinian cause and the Palestinian revolution, not to generate profit.

The best way to distribute Palestinian films was to screen them on Arab television channels; however, Palestinian cinema generally remained at the mercy of the Palestine revolution's relationship with Arab governments. Later, toward the end of the 1970s, a few Arab TV channels bought copies of these films. Among them were those of Algeria, Kuwait, and Qatar.

ATTEMPTS AT UNIFYING FILMMAKING EFFORTS

A first initiative for unification came from the Palestine Film Unit, where Mustafa faced difficulty garnering appreciation from the political leadership for cinema's role in the revolution, especially after leaving Jordan in 1970 and arriving in Lebanon. He began to feel a contradiction or tension between the vision of the filmmakers, especially in relation to the artistic styles of the film, and the conventional styles of journalists. He presented a project for unifying filmmaking efforts because he felt that these challenges may be experienced by other filmmakers working as part of information and news departments of Palestinian political organizations that were affiliated with the PLO.

Hassan Abu Ghanimeh[40] explained the first unification initiative:

[40] Abu Ghanimeh, *Palestine and the Cinematic Eye*, p. 266–274.

The filmmaker Mustafa Abu Ali was the first to pose the question of unifying the efforts of filmmakers in Palestinian movements in a project he called "Palestine Films" in 1972. The project aimed to establish a general Palestinian Cinema Institution. In presenting the project, he said "Establishing an institute for Palestinian cinema is an important effort that will be a mark in history. Whoever will support this project will place the foundational rock giving the green light for a history of Palestinian cinema. Supporting the project of a Palestinian cinema institution is supporting the Palestinian revolution and the cause of the Palestinian people. Establishing an institute like this is a historical responsibility that must be fulfilled by all those who believe in the cause of the Palestinian people."

Abu Ghanimeh further noted:

The Palestine Film Unit was established as part of Fatah's information efforts, and Fatah was, at the time, the first to be interested in this important populist tool, cinema. It first established a department of photography, and provided some basic filmmaking equipment later, and recruited thirteen people to work in the department since 1968. The unit was keen, upon leaving Jordan, on taking its equipment and film footage with it. However, parts of the Fatah leadership, who made decisions after the events of Black September in 1970, felt like the revolutionary conditions were not suitable for cinema production. As such, we call for the establishment of a Palestinian cinema institution, which builds on our four years of experience.

Abu Ghanimeh described the financial and material obstacles that justified creating a new film institute that would unify "efforts and capabilities to continue producing films that experiment and search for a special experimental militant language."

He also outlined the commitments of this project to making films that cover the revolution's military and political activities, as well as the conditions of the Palestinian people in their places of residence, and revolutionary activities across the Arab world and beyond. The institute would produce films that serve the Palestinian revolution and its people, and the Arab revolution. It would work to distribute its films and produce more of them. It would establish an archive of its films and of other films about the Palestinian cause, in addition to training personnel and participating in international festivals. The project also addressed the nature of the films, their production mechanisms, budgets, the structure of missions, the stages of the institute's development, and the responsibilities of those who work for the institute. The institute's staff would comprise a steering council, an administrative employee, a director, a cinematographer, a photography department, an editor, a sound engineer, and an onsite filming crew.[41]

The proposal was considered, but given the circumstances at the time, the project's implementation was postponed.

Abu Ghanimeh elaborated:

> The project did not materialize. However, the issue of unifying the cinema initiatives of the various Palestinian organizations and institutes was a concern for all filmmakers. This sentiment was expressed by all who participated in the first session of the symposium[42] held at the [office of the] *Palestine Affairs* on the topic of cinema and the Palestinian cause. The symposium was administered by the researcher Hani Hourani,[43] who edited and published its proceedings. Participants included the critic Walid Chmait, the director Qasem Hawal, the director Mustafa Abu Ali, the critic Ibrahim Zayer.[44]

The first session of the symposium discussed unifying the cinema initiatives of the various Palestinian organizations and institutes under the PLO. The participants agreed to the importance of establishing a single body for film production, but they disagreed on the name. Some preferred calling it a collective rather than an institute. This perhaps explains the name Palestinian Cinema Group (PCG) which was used, at the end of 1972, to describe the efforts to establish a unified cinema initiative to support filmmaking away from the political and ideological differences of the various organizations working with filmmaking, and their understanding of the role of cinema.

---

[41] Ibid., p. 268–270.

[42] *Palestine Affairs* [magazine], tenth edition, June 1972. It was republished in the edited volume *Palestine in Cinema*, by Walid Chmait and Guy Hennebelle, 1977, by the Palestinian Ministry of Culture in 2006.

[43] Hani Hourani, economic and political researcher, worked at the Palestine Research Center in the 1970s. He served as the editor-in-chief of the magazine *Al-Urdon Al-Jadeed* in the 1980s and established the Al-Urdon Al-Jadeed Studies Center in the 1990s. He is a writer, a researcher, and a fine artist.

[44] Ibrahim Zayer, an Iraqi journalist, critic, and poet, was born in the city of Al-Amarah in 1944. He lived a hard life after the Arab defeat in the 1967 war and joined the Palestinian revolution in 1970.

A FILMMAKER EMERGES FROM THE RANKS
OF THE MILITANTS

In the second half of 1972, Mustafa returned from a visit to the military bases in Southern Lebanon, very pleased to have found a young Iraqi fighter, Samir Nimr, who claimed to have experience in filmmaking. Mustafa would ask the leadership to transfer him from military duty to work with the Palestine Film Unit.

The Iraqi Filmmaker/Cinematographer, Samir Nimr (Real Name: Farid Ahmad Al-Sheikh)

We were happy to have found Samir Nimr, a militant who also had experience in filmmaking, especially since I was the only one available to occasionally help Mustafa.

Samir Nimr was a young Iraqi who was shocked by the Arab defeat in 1967. Once he learned of the establishment of the Palestinian Fedayee movement, he asked around and eventually joined the training camp in Iraq which took in volunteers wanting to become fedayeen. He went on to join the fedayee bases in Southern Lebanon.

We rarely spoke about ourselves or shared intimate details of our lives, as if life before the revolution was no longer relevant. Or perhaps we continued living in the secrecy that was necessary in the early days of working with the revolution. I did not come to know Samir personally or learn about his previous experiences except through his interview with the Lebanese writer and critic Walid Chmait, who had worked with the French critic Guy Hennbelle on the book *Palestine in Cinema*.

Chmait described Samir as follows:

He was interested in photography and cinema since he was in school. With his classmates, he made two films about the revolution in Iraq in 1958 entitled *With Dawn* and *The Will of the People*. Before joining the Iraqi Television, he participated in two narrative films, *The Happiest Days* (which was never completed), and *The Path of Love*, where he worked as assistant cinematographer and editor, as well as acting in the film.[45]

However, Samir admits that he truly found himself through Palestinian cinema. He details his experiences in the interview, noting:

[45] Walid Chmait and Guy Hennebelle, *Palestine in Cinema*, 1977, republished by Palestinian Ministry of Culture in 2006. NP

Fig. 4.3   The filmmaker/cinematographer Samir Nimr

The directions were very clear. Film everything and save it as political documentation. We filmed all the events of the war [in Lebanon], no matter how small or big. We moved with our cameras from one direction to the other, from one battle to the next. We helped foreign correspondents and some progressive filmmaking colleagues who came from various news agencies and tv channels. Some of them used to give us copies of what they had filmed in east Beirut.[46] (Fig. 4.3)

A New Photography Department for the Palestine Film Unit in Beirut

There was a great need for photographers in the Palestine Film Unit in Beirut in the absence of the founders Sulafa and Hani and after many photographers had left for Baghdad from Damascus for cinematography workshops. This need was increased by the departure of the photography department for Damascus, where they were engaged with covering events and activities in Syria.

[46] Ibid. NP.

Memories of Photographer Mahmoud Nofal[47]

"I was alone at the beginning of 1973. I was injured during the events of Black September, sent to Czechoslovakia for treatment and completed my recovery in Cairo. When I joined the photography department there was a foreigner called Bruno[48] who worked between the photography and the film department. He taught me how to develop and print in the dark room. As there was high demand for photographs, I suggested recruiting brother Ibrahim Al-Msadar, who was from Deir Al-Balah. I met him in Cairo where we were both receiving treatment alongside others who were injured on the revolution's battlefield.

"Ibrahim Al-Msadar is a militant who had joined the movement in Gaza and was injured there. When he joined the photography department, he was also trained in photography and printing by Bruno, though he took on more of an administrative role. After about seven months Hasan Al-Kharouf also joined the photography department, in early 1974. Hasan was from Acre and was sent for treatment in Beirut after being injured during the Al-Karameh Battle. Because he enjoyed photography, he photographed for the Palestinian Red Crescent while he received treatment. Afterwards he joined the photography department of the Palestine Film Unit."

At the beginning, the photographers in Beirut were injured militants who were transferred to the Palestine Film Unit for training in the photography department after they could no longer engage in combat.

Mahmoud Nofal added: "The young militant Yousef Qutob joined us through the brother Majed Abu Sharar who took over the Unified Information Office in 1974. Yousef was interested in photography and asked brother Majed to be transferred to train and work with us. The four of us became the Photography Department."

Yousef Qutob was born in Jerusalem and joined Fatah as a young man. He was injured in the battles of Black September in 1970. While he was receiving treatment in the hospital, Majed Abu Sharar, who was his relative, was surprised to find a camera next to him, and he learned that Yousef

---

[47] Interview with Mahmoud Nofal, a Palestinian militant born in Hebron in 1951, conducted by the author on October 17, 2017.

[48] Bruno, a photographer, possibly Italian, used to cooperate with Fatah's Information Office in Lebanon. I was not able to learn his full name from those he taught or obtain any additional information about him. Militants did not share any private information with each other, due to the need for secrecy.

Fig. 4.4 Photographers of the new department: from right Mahmoud Nofal, Ibrahim Msadar, Hasan Al Kharouf, Yousef Al Qutob, 1976

was interested in photography. Yousef joined the department as soon as he left the hospital (Fig. 4.4).

By 1973, the PFU in Lebanon had two departments. The first was the film department where Mustafa Abu Ali worked as director with Samir Nimr as cinematographer in the beginning and then later joined by Omar Mukhtar after his return from training in Baghdad. The second was the photography department with the four above-mentioned people (Mahmoud Noufal, Ibrahim Al-Msadar, Hassan Al Kharouf, Yousef Al-Qutb). The photography department used to cover all the activities including events, visiting delegations, and everything that happened in the Palestinian arena.

In 1974, after the establishment of the Unified Information Office, there was another attempt to propose the unification project, and a committee including filmmakers and critics was established composed of Mustafa Abu Ali (Palestine Film Unit/Fatah), Ismael Shammout (Department of Culture and Art/PLO), Qasem Hawal (Committee of Central Information/Arts Section/PFLP), Rafiq Hajjar (Artistic Committee/DFLP), Hassan Abu Ghanimeh (critic and researcher), and a

Fig. 4.5 The new logo of the Palestinian Cinema Institution

representative of the Unified Information Office. The committee met several times but nothing came of it.

This is how the PFU adopted the unification project itself, and its name became the Palestinian Cinema Institution (Fig. 4.5).

BIBLIOGRAPHY

Abu Ali, Khadijeh. "Al-'Arud al- Sinima'iyah wa Bidayatuha" ["Film Screenings and their Beginnings"]. *Al-Surah al-Filastiniyah [Palestinian Image]*. Second issue, March 1979, Beirut: Muassaset al-Sinima al-Filastiniyah, p. 31-35.

Abu Ali, Mustafa and Hassan Abu Ghanimeh. *An al-Sinima al-Filastiniyah [About the Palestinian Cinema]*. Beirut: Wihdet Aflam Filastin /Muassaset al-Sinima al-Filastiniyah, 1975.

Abu Ghanimeh, Hassan. *Filastin wa-al'Ayn al-Sinima'I [Palestine and the Cinematic Eye]*. Damascus: Ittihad al-Kuttab al-'Arab, 1981.

Chmait, Walid and Guy Hennebelle, eds. *Filastin fi al-Sinima [Palestine in Cinema]*, 2nd ed. Ramallah: Wizarat al-Thaqafah al-Filastiniyah, al-Hay'ah al-'Ammah al-Filastiniyah lil Kitab, 2006.

Oudat, Husayn al-. *Al-Sinima wa-al Qadiyah al-Filastiniyah [Cinema and the Palestinian Cause]*. Damascus: Al-Ahali. 1987

Robledo, Pablo. *Montoneros Y Palestina: De la Revolution a La Dictadura [Montoneros and Palestine: From Revolution to Dictatorship]*. Buenos Aires: Editorial Planeta, 2018.

CHAPTER 5

From Palestine Film Unit to Palestinian Cinema Institution

After the Palestine Film Unit (PFU) became known as the Palestinian Cinema Institution (PCI), more effort was channeled into developing it to include more people working in the different technical areas of filmmaking. The PCI received some aide from ally states including East Germany, the Soviet Union, Iraq, Libya, and Cuba, to cover filmmaking equipment and scholarships for training in the various aspects of film production. All of this participated in the development of the PCI, which also expanded to include more departments, specializing in cinematography, photography, filming and documenting current events, producing seasonal newsreels and films, and adding jointly produced films with progressive filmmakers visiting from the Arab countries, Europe, Asia, and Latin America. Such film productions about the Palestinian cause became a phenomenon in world cinema.

Attempts at Producing a Narrative Film

Around the end of 1972 and beginning of 1973, after the network of relations of the Unit had expanded, and several documentary films and newsreels were produced, Mustafa, by now the PFU's head and main director, started to feel the need to produce narrative films. He wanted to reach the larger audiences who did not watch documentary films and felt that narrative films touch and express the more human aspects of the Palestinian

K. Habashneh, *Knights of Cinema*, Palgrave Studies in Arab Cinema, https://doi.org/10.1007/978-3-031-18858-9_5

experience, ranging from the Nakba of 1948 to the life of the Palestinian people in exile and under occupation. He also wanted to express his own humanitarian values through an artistic cinematic language.

Mustafa prepared a script for a fiction film based on the novel *The Days of Love and Death* by Palestinian author Rashad Abu Shawer, which narrates a love story during the war of 1948 and the catastrophe that ensued.

Abu Shawer recalls, "Mustafa called and invited me to Beirut – I had been living in Damascus at the time – and he informed me that he had read my novel *The Days of Love and Death* published in 1973. He was excited to adapt it to a film and had received approval from the leadership.

"Mustafa prepared a working draft of the script while I assisted him. I learned the art of crafting and combining scenes for the script along the way. Then, he submitted the draft of the scenario to the Algerian Cinema Institute, and they enthusiastically agreed to co-produce the film.

"My second novel *Tears on a Lovers Chest* was published in 1974, and all hell broke loose over the criticism it contained of the rampant shortcomings of the revolution. A powerful Palestinian entity was sent to the Algerian Cinema Institute to halt work on the film.

"Mustafa was surprised by the reaction. He relayed the news of the cancellation of *The Days of Love and Death* with sorrow and bitterness. I recall him asking, 'Couldn't you have postponed publishing your novel until next year?'

"It had not occurred to me at the time that you [Mustafa] would be punished for the publication of my novel, as they had thought I was the one being punished.

"Mustafa became preoccupied with transforming the cinema department in the Palestinian Information Office (of the Palestine Film Unit) into an institute with technical expertise and a number of photographers, directors, and filmmakers, with the necessary equipment to produce films through Palestinian and Arab efforts. He also invested in sending personnel to training courses, conferences, and forums that increased their knowledge and experience."[1]

The same situation occurred at the beginning of the 1980s with the film *The Pessoptimist (Al Mutashail)* adapted from Emile Habibi's novel *Saeed Abu Al Nahs Al Mutashail (The Secret Life of Saeed: The Pessoptimist)*.

---

[1] From Rashad Abu Shawer's introduction to our self-published script of *Al-Mutashail* (*The Pessoptimist)* written by Mustafa Abu Ali presented and distributed to the Palestine Cinema Days film festival at FilmLab in Ramallah, October 2014, p. 7–8.

The idea of adaptation was met with surprise, as the dominant opinion among the intellectuals of the revolution was that it was impossible to turn the novel into a film because of its formal nature that relies on ambiguous language and thinly veiled sarcasm. They were very surprised when Mustafa prepared the script and received approval from the author Emile Habibi, who expressed great admiration for the work. Mustafa recalls that Habibi had not expected to see a film adaptation of his novel and was pleased with the additions that the adaptation made to the original text, referring to the closing scene where Mustafa places Yacoub, the Eastern Jew, and Saeed, the Palestinian, each on a separate pole, standing back-to-back, unable to see each other.

Amid the astonishment of the cultural and intellectual cadres, and their admiration for the script, the film received approval to be produced in 1979/1980.

Upon Mustafa's request, I personally reached out to the director Mustafa Al-Aqqad[2] to join the production team and presented Mustafa's script of *The Pessoptimist* when I visited London in early 1980. While there, I finished my film *Children Without Childhood* by adding finishing artistic touches that had not been available at Studio Al-Sakhra in Beirut. Mustafa also presented the project to the Palestinian economist Abdel Mohsin Al-Qattan,[3] who deeply appreciated the novel and expressed his interest in funding the production. The script was also translated into French and sent to the French researcher and consultant Rene Thevenet in 1979. Thevenet conducted a feasibility study that guided the appeal to French producers. His report anticipated a high probability of success.

Unfortunately, after the 1982 war, funding allocated for the film was diverted to other more pressing concerns of the revolution. The slashed funding proved to be a demoralizing blow for Mustafa who had taken major steps toward the accomplishment of the work. He had already pre-pared contracts for co-productions with states like Algeria and Tunisia. In addition, Mustafa and I were hosted for more than two weeks in Tunis after the Carthage Days of Cinema in October 1980 to research and scout locations. Several actors had also been contacted, including the Syrian

---

[2] Mustafa Al-Aqqad, an American film director and producer of Syrian origin, worked in Hollywood and directed the films *The Message* (1976) and *Lion of the Desert* (1981), also known as *Omar Al-Mukhtar.*

[3] Abdel Mohsin Al-Qattan, a well-known Palestinian businessman and economist, is one of the founders of Taawon, an organization dedicated to supporting and funding Palestinian cultural projects.

actor Doraid Lahham for the role of Saeed Abu Al-Nahs, the Pessoptimist, and the Egyptian actor Izzat Al-Alayli for the role of the big man, among others. The experience preparing for this film is perhaps itself worthy of a film.

Had this failure to realize the importance of the film been limited to the political leadership, we would have excused them for the nature of the challenges, pressures, and conspiracies they confronted. However, the shortsightedness and failure to realize the importance of cinema carried over to influential decision-makers among the culture and the information leadership. Some believed that the production of *The Pessoptimist* was not tactical because the main character of the film is a Palestinian who collaborates with the occupation. They most likely did not read the script or pay attention to the ending where the main character sees himself in a dream being suspended on a pole.

ESTABLISHING THE PALESTINIAN CINEMA GROUP (PCG)

Since the early days of the Palestine Film Unit in Lebanon and Mustafa's hardships trying to assert the role of cinema in the revolution, he had been thinking about the need for a framework that joins filmmakers working with the revolution. He presented the project of unifying filmmaking groups under the PLO in 1972 and was unsuccessful.

Mustafa returned once more to conceptualize a framework for Palestinian and Arab filmmakers and intellectuals working with the revolution and in support of its struggle. The idea was presented at the Damascus International Festival for Youth Cinema in April 1972. A number of filmmakers who had participated in the festival joined to discuss the project, including Samir Farid and Fouad Al-Tuhami from Egypt, Hamid Bannani from Morocco, Abdelaziz Telbi from Algeria, Qasem Hawal and Abdelhadi Al-Rawi from Iraq, and Hassan Abu-Ghanimeh and Adnan Madanat from Jordan, among others. An initial version of a statement was drafted.

Conversations took place at the Fourth International Carthage Film Festival toward the end of 1972, where a manifesto was released by Arab filmmakers for the support of Palestinian revolutionary cinema. The writers and critics Al-Taher Cheriaa and Abdelkarim Qabous from Tunis, among others, participated in the above-mentioned Arab filmmakers' manifesto.

The main idea behind the establishment of the group was to develop a unifying framework for filmmakers that would provide greater freedom to express artistic visions. The framework would distance filmmakers from

the hegemony of Palestinian political groups in decision-making, which Mustafa began to view as a hurdle to the development of Palestinian cinema and the search for different cinematic language in revolutionary films.

The group was established with approximately 35 filmmakers and intellectuals from Palestine and the Arab World, including the well-known Egyptian director Tawfiq Saleh,[4] Jordanian journalist and film critic Hassan Abu Ghanimeh,

Palestinian militant and writer Daoud Talhami, Iraqi filmmaker and militant Qasem Hawal, Jordanian filmmaker and writer Adnan Madanat, Palestinian journalist Rasmi Abu Ali, Palestinian researcher and writer Issam Sakhnini, Jordanian militant and writer Nazeeh Abu Nidal, and Khadijeh Habashneh Abu Ali (myself), joined them, among others.

Hassan Abu Ghanimeh Described the Establishment of the PCG in Palestine and the Cinematic Eye

"An administrative body for the group was elected. Mustafa Abu Ali was the General Secretary, Issam Sakhnini (representative of the Palestine Research Center) was the treasurer, Tawfiq Saleh and Hassan Abu-Ghanimeh were members."

He elaborated: "The main idea that the group agreed on was that cinema must be a real, effective weapon in service of the liberation of the Palestinian nation and its people. After several meetings and discussions, the basic principles of the group were drafted:

1. We must continue documenting and making films about revolutionary activities.
2. We must exert cautious effort and attention to collecting photographic and written historical documents about Palestine and the Zionist movement.
3. We must expand and strengthen collaboration between the Palestinian Cinema Group and other revolutionary movements in Africa, Asia and Latin America, and other movements globally.

---

[4] Tawfiq Saleh, an Egyptian writer and filmmaker, had a new, progressive vision for cinema. This was demonstrated in his critical films including *Darb Al Mahabeel (Fools' Road)* which he collaborated on with Egyptian novelist Najib Mahfouz in 1955, and *The Rebels* and *Struggles of Heroes* which forced him to leave Egypt and live in exile in Syria. There, he made *The Dupes*, adapted from Ghassan Kanafani's novella *Men in the Sun*, produced by the General Cinema Institute in Damascus 1972.

The Palestine Research Center, which operates under the PLO, helped us establish the Palestinian Cinema Group (PCG) by offering us a place to work and fully endorsing our basic principles."[5]

The PCG also affirmed its total commitment to the decisions of the PLO and the general political attitude of the Palestinian resistance and the revolution.

The official birth of the group was in November 1972, upon the return of the Palestinian delegation from the Fourth Carthage Days of Cinema Festival. The delegation presented a report to the leadership of the PLO and the Palestine Research Center about their first participation in an international film festival alongside the African revolutionary movements.

The PCG was adopted by the Palestine Research Center headed by Professor Anis Al-Sayigh.[6] The group received space and funding for a short film (no longer than 12 minutes) entitled *Scenes from the Occupation of Gaza*. It was the first colored 35 mm film at the time (the full story will be told later). During their participation in the Baghdad International Festival for Films and Programs on Palestine, the group published the first statement expressing its vision for militant cinema and its role in national liberation.[7] The group's delegation to the festival included Mustafa Abu-Ali, Hassan Abu Ghanimeh, and others.

The group's first film won the golden prize at the festival, but Mustafa notes that this was ultimately to their disadvantage. The success of the group provoked conservatives among the political leadership to assert that cinema belonged under the Unified Information Office, not the Palestine Research Center. They asked that the research center revoke its support for the group. Mustafa initially resisted the idea of returning to the Unified Information Office, although after a series of deliberations and conversations, he became affiliated again to the office of Palestine Film under the umbrella of the Unified Information Office. However, this was in name only, as every Palestinian organization retained its own information office and cinema committee.

---

[5] Hassan Abu Ghanimeh. *Palestine and the Cinematic Eye* (Damascus: Union of Arab Writers, 1981), p. 263–266.

[6] Anis Al-Sayigh is a Palestinian writer and head of the Palestine Research Center. He has published numerous books about the history of Palestine and the Palestinian cause.

[7] The text of the statement is found in Appendix A.

SCENES FROM THE OCCUPATION OF GAZA

This film has a very specific story, as the Palestine Film Unit received some footage filmed in Occupied Palestine from a European television crew that had relations with the unit, which sometimes exchanged film footage or facilitated meetings with the leadership. The material received was from Gaza, the most revolutionary city in Occupied Palestine in the early 1970s. Mustafa was very pleased with the material as he started brainstorming ways of using it in a film about the life of the Palestinian people in Gaza under occupation. However, the European television crew who shot this footage were accompanied by Occupation forces. This meant that the behavior of the Zionist soldiers was less violent, or at least slightly more considerate in these circumstances, and as such, the footage can be considered as promoting the behavior of the occupying soldiers. The material arrived and the production of the film began shortly after the establishment of the Palestinian Cinema Group and its adoption by the Palestine Research Center.

Mustafa was excited by the material for two reasons: firstly, because it was from Gaza, a place he could not reach to express the life and struggle of the Palestinian people in an explosive city of Palestinian resistance. Secondly, the material allowed him the chance to experiment with the idea of repurposing images filmed for a different purpose and using them artistically to serve a different goal. The film employed a very special cinematic language that had been unusual at the time, as Mustafa narrated through the eyes of Gazans the anger of the revolution that dwelled in their souls but was kept hidden from the enemy. He represented their struggle through the reports of news agencies, quotes from the enemy's leadership, and the revolution's broadcasting channel.

The Film's Style and its Critical Recognition

Mustafa described his style used in the film: "As I watched the material, my role was to closely read the images, to touch the reality captured in people's eyes. It was as if I were underlining and highlighting important passages of a text. Then I added my cinematic annotations. I would see the revolution through our peoples' eyes as they tried to conceal their emotions in front of the camera. Because the original material of the film gave a positive impression of the nature of the occupation and the resistance in Gaza, I chose to work with only 8 minutes of the original 20-minute French reportage clip.

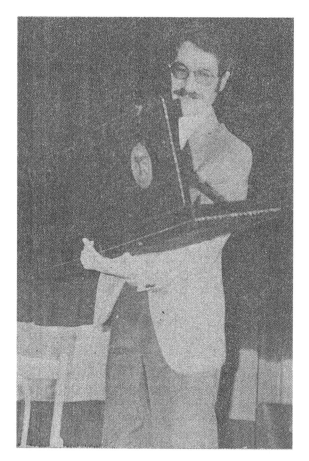

Fig. 5.1   Mustafa Abu Ali receives the Golden prize for *Scenes from the Occupation of Gaza,* Baghdad International Festival for Films and TV Programs, March 1973

"I built on the available film material with my original cinematic language, as I tried to fight the enemy with its own weapons."[8] (Fig. 5.1)

In his book, Abu Ghanimeh quotes several responses to demonstrate the high regard with which this film was met. Fouad Al-Tuhami, one of the famous Arab documentary filmmakers, describes the film: "The director of the film is engaged with the struggle and is fluent in its revolutionary

[8] Abu Ghanimeh, *Palestine and the Cinematic Eye,* p. 331–332.

language. When he received this documentary material, he chose from it the scenes that best expressed the revolution as he encountered it."[9]

The revolutionary Indian director Mrinal Sen described the film at the Tashkent Film Festival:

"This film is a live example of a cinema supporting a people's war ... a cinema that possesses its own weapons derived from a full understanding of the criteria of a long-term people's war. It is exemplary of a process of seizing the enemy's weapon and using it against him on the battlefield."[10]

The film was screened at the First Baghdad International Festival for Films and TV Programs on Palestine in 1973 where it won the golden prize. It was followed by a panel on Palestinian cinema which discussed the importance of integrating the revolution and revolutionaries in Palestinian films. The Palestinian Cinema Group also published its first statement where it affirmed the importance of Palestinian cinema, and the necessity for supporting its development in order to stand alongside the brave militant fighters.[11]

THEY DO NOT EXIST: A DIFFERENT CINEMATIC LANGUAGE

Mustafa's belief in the necessity of making a narrative film was disrupted when the Nabatieh refugee camp was targeted by brutal bombardment and shelling by the Israeli Air Force in May 1974, which led to the destruction of three quarters of the camp.

In response, he began working on the film *They Do Not Exist* that subverts Golda Meir's famous saying: "Who are the Palestinians? I have never heard this word before. They do not exist."

The film records the genocidal operation that fell upon Nabatieh camp in May 1974. It builds upon an unfamiliar structure of documentary filmmaking comprised of nine segments. Unprecedented shots of the barbaric Israeli Air Force bombardment are superimposed over music composed by Johann Sebastian Bach.

When the film was screened at the Leipzig International Film Festival in 1974, it was well received for its message and unique cinematic language. However, it spurred a wide debate about the director's use of music by Bach, among the most famous European composers, alongside

[9] Ibid., p. 333.
[10] Ibid., p. 334.
[11] The text of the statement is found in Appendix A.

footage of Israeli bombardment of the camp. Despite this, the film received an honorary mention at Leipzig, and went on to win the Arab critic's prize at the Carthage Days of Cinema Festival in 1975.

It is said that this is the most widely requested and viewed Palestinian film.

Director and Researcher Qais Al-Zubaidi Writes About Mustafa's Cinematic Experience[12]

"Through his films, Mustafa Abu Ali has shown us what cinema means as an audio-visual medium. Through his experimenting with various elements of image and sound, Mustafa asserts that the plot of a film unfolds through both the audio and the visual elements. In *They Do Not Exist*, we see how he employs audio and video to invoke both simultaneity and dissonance. We also see how he employs commentary, interviews, music, anthem, and song, as elements that complement, contradict, critique, or simply stand in the background of the image.

After some research, it is fair to say that most of Mustafa Abu Ali's films are not simply a theoretical exercise in cinema. Rather, they are often artistic writing through film, as opposed to theory printed on paper."[13]

HANI JAWHARIEH'S RETURN

In October 1975, Hani was finally able to obtain a passport and arrived in Beirut to join the Palestinian Cinema Institution. He had been among the core members of the Palestine Film Unit established in 1968, where he captured footage and prepared for the first film *No to a Peaceful Solution* in 1969.

Hani arrived around mid-October 1975, and I recall the reunion in our house as if it were yesterday. It seems that he arrived at the institute while I was not there, but I remember he came over for lunch. After eating, we were drinking our coffee, when Mustafa said:

> By God, welcome back Abu Alfakher. You've been delayed for so long. But here you are, and I desperately need you because I'm tired of doing this fight alone. Brother, you have to take over the administration of the institute

---

[12] Qais Al-Zubaidi, an Iraqi leftist militant, directed several documentaries about the Palestinian cause. He is also a researcher and film critic.

[13] Al-Zubaidi, "From Revolution to Cinema," an unpublished paper written in preparation for a panel on the fiftieth anniversary of the first Palestinian film, September 2019, which was postponed due to political demonstrations in Lebanon at the time.

from now on. I just want to be a director. You are better than I at dealing with these politicians.

Hani replied: "Oh no, brother. After all this work establishing a well-respected institute, you want me to take over the management? Brother, I am a cinematographer, not an administrator."

Mustafa tried to convince him, but Hani completely refused, and Mustafa accepted:

Ok. But don't jump ahead to film every battle you hear about. We now have a number of photographers for news and documentation. You're an artistically inclined cinematographer and your role should be in fiction films. We've made documentaries, and everyone is making them. Now it's time for us to make a fiction film.

Hani and Mustafa both wanted free time to concentrate on their work, while each tried to pin the administrative duties on the other. Neither of them was interested in the responsibilities of a managerial post. This was one of the characteristics of the revolutionary militants at the time (Fig. 5.2).

Fig. 5.2 A rare picture of Hani and Mustafa at the Baghdad International Festival for Palestinian Films and TV programs, March 1976

HANI'S MARTYRDOM AND COMMEMORATIONS

Unfortunately, we did not celebrate Hani's return for very long. He was fatally wounded while covering one of the battles of Aintoura hills on April 11, 1976. His martyrdom shortly after his return was harrowing and painful for his friends at the PCI and for everyone who knew him (Fig. 5.3).

However, Hani left a special mark on everyone at the PCI for his tireless and selfless work. He had managed, after his return, to convince the militant filmmaker Sulafa Jadallah to come to Beirut to work at the PCI. Together, they established an administrative system to organize cinematic and documentary filming of events, popular activities, and leadership movements (Fig. 5.4). They also developed a training plan that benefited filmmakers from the institute including brothers from Yemen and Eritrea who learned filmmaking there. During his short time in Beirut, Hani filmed two works—*On the Road to Victory* directed by Mustafa in 1975 and produced by the PCI, and *The Key* directed by Ghaleb Sha'ath[14] in 1976 which was produced by the SAMED Institute for Cinematic Production.

Mustafa recalled Hani's martyrdom in his article "The Martyr of Palestinian Cinema":[15]

"On April 9th, 1976, Hani accompanies a delegation of Fatah leaders to the mountains (Aintoura, Al-Zarour, Sineen), some of the highest areas in Lebanon. The joint Palestinian-Lebanese forces took over the area because of its strategic importance in fighting the right-wing forces. The area was seized at the beginning of 1976 when snow on the mountains stood higher than 20 cm. In April, some of the snow had melted but a considerable amount remained. The mountain was studded with mounds of pure white snow shining under bright rays of sun, and the spirit of the revolution among the fighters captured Hani's imagination. The Fatah delegation returned after inspecting the site, but Hani stayed behind. He roamed around the mountain, moving from one base to another with his 16 mm camera, carefully framing the shots he captured.

---

[14] Ghaleb Sha'ath, a Palestinian film director, studied in Vienna, where he received a diploma in engineering in 1963, and a diploma in film directing from the Cinema Institute in 1967. He worked in Egyptian cinema and participated in establishing the New Cinema Group in Egypt in 1968, where he directed the film *Shadows on the Other Side* (1974).

[15] Mustafa Abu Ali, "The Martyr of Palestinian Cinema," in *Palestinian Image* magazine, First Issue, November (Beirut: Palestinian Cinema Institution, 1978), p. 16–17.

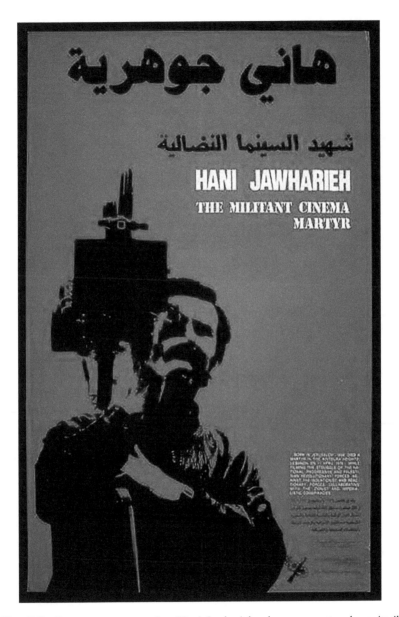

Fig. 5.3   Poster commemorating Hani Jawharieh who was martyred on April 11, 1976

Fig. 5.4 Sulafa Jadallah and Hani Jawharieh at the Palestinian Cinema Institution, 1976

"The right-wing shelling of the area did not stop, as the brother accompanying Hani informed me, but Hani insisted on recording everything.

"On April 11th, at around three o'clock in the evening, a rocket landed half a meter away from Hani. Was his camera filming as the rocket fell? Did Hani film the moment of his martyrdom? We have no way of knowing, because the camera was also martyred and the film inside was destroyed."

Our grief over losing Hani was stronger than our joy for his return. We all had great expectations, but his friend Mustafa especially felt the loss as he was starting to be exasperated by documentary filmmaking and was planning for his feature fiction film. Hani had been Mustafa's spiritual equal in the artistic universe. His transparent sense of how to capture a meaningful and expressive shot made him a true-born cinematographer.

Mustafa wrote in "Hani as Cinematographer":[16]

Full immersion is different from detailed expression. While executing a specific shot, Hani would become a part of it. A part of its rhythm and movement, a part of the event's visceral sensibility. All of this would translate
into film.

Mustafa continued offering descriptions of Hani's filming of the militants and the people during the revolution's work in Jordan. He added in
the same article: "Man always came first, and the weapon came second.
The union of man and his weapon is what Hani expressed in all his works
on the Palestinian Revolution."

Commemorating Hani Jawharieh (1939–1976)

Hani's martyrdom was a painful blow not just to members of the institute,
but also to all members of the various information departments. News of
his death spread widely, as some sources described him as the first filmmaker to be martyred on the battlefield since World War II. The week
following his death, the magazine *Palestine of the Revolution* (*Falastin
Al-Thawra*) prepared a special edition on Hani and his works, including
testimonies from friends like Mustafa, Mutee', Muwafaq, and myself. A
number of the revolution's leadership including Majed Abu Sharar, Sakher
Habash, and Yahya Rabah also contributed. From the ranks of Palestinian
and Arab artists and poets came testimonies from Muna Saudi, Mu'een
Bseiso, Ezzeddine Al-Manassara, Walid Chmait, Adnan Madanat, and
Rasmi Abu Ali.

On January 1, 1977, for the anniversary of the birth of the revolution,
the photography department at the PCI set up an exhibition of Hani's
works, showing a number of the photographs that the martyr had captured during different stages of the revolution. Mustafa's only act of
mourning after the martyrdom was directing a film about Hani's life and
works entitled *Palestine in the Eye* 1977. He refused to submit it to com-
pete in any festivals, considering it was a tribute to the spirit of his friend
Hani. The PCI established a prize in Hani Jawharieh's name to be awarded
at Arab and international festivals for best films in support of the Palestinian

---

[16] Mustafa Abu Ali, "Hani as Cinematographer," in *Palestinian Image* magazine, Second
Issue, November (Beirut: Palestinian Cinema Institution, 1979), p. 11–12.

cause or other popular revolution around the world. The first prize was awarded at the Carthage Days of Cinema in 1978 to *Los Hijos De Fierro* by the Argentinian director Fernando Pino Solanas. The film shows the struggle and resistance of the popular movement in Argentina.

The Tunisian Ministry of Culture also named one of the largest cinemas on Al-Habib Bourguiba Street in the capital Tunis in the name of the Martyr Hani Jawharieh. In addition, the training sessions at the institute were named after Hani, as graduate certificates for training courses also bore his name. There were also small and large posters, and a collection of Hani's photographs as a gift to friends and to the visitors of the revolution's institutions.

The commemoration of Hani Jawharieh became a real addition to the work of the institute.

SCENES FROM CHALLENGING WORKING CONDITIONS

Work at the PFU/PCI was not easy, as challenging conditions persisted. Mustafa describes these conditions in his article "Snapshots of the Cinema Experience During the Lebanese War":[17]

> At the very beginning of the war, the team responded to the major events. It was initially a Lebanese war, and as the person in charge, I knew this. So did the rest of the team. This awareness reflected our activities that aligned with the ideals of the struggle. As long as the struggle was Lebanese, it was better expressed by the Lebanese themselves. As long as we were allies, as a revolutionary movement, with the progressive and nationalist Lebanese organizations we were best off giving these groups a chance to express the war cinematically. From this perspective, the institute worked with the Lebanese Communist Party on a film about the war. However, it faltered because there were no available filmmakers working with the party. At the same time, parallel work initially conceptualized by the Lebanese filmmaker Randa Chahal resulted in the film *Step by Step*, released in 1977.

Mustafa continues in the same article:

"The war became increasingly dangerous, as people started to feel anxious walking down the street. What if a rocket suddenly landed next to

---

[17] Mustafa Abu Ali, "Snapshots of the Cinematic Experience During the Lebanese War (1975-1976)," in *Palestinian Image* magazine, First issue, November (Beirut: Palestinian Cinema Institution, 1978), p. 16–19.

them? They sit at home afraid that a rocket would land and puncture the wall. During wartime, no place is safe from the rockets. People would exchange humorous stories, perhaps to ease their anxiety about how a rocket dropped between two buildings, each 40m in height and 0.5m apart, or perhaps how the rocket landed in this narrow space, killing everyone on the second floor.

"We were astonished by such occurrences, but they definitely happened, and they spread an air of anxiety and insecurity. One day I was with a friend from the institute. We carried our equipment as we walked down a street in Al-Shayyah area. Suddenly, I saw my friend throw himself, like an arrow, to lay vertically on the floor of a building entrance.... I looked at him surprised and curious, but he did not return my gaze. He joined his hands above his head as he lay on the ground. I quickly understood that he was taking the necessary self-defense precautions during aerial bombardment. I froze for a second, then I burst out laughing. My friend rose, asking whether the rocket had exploded.

I replied, 'What are you talking about?'

He said, 'I heard the rocket dropping.'

Me: 'But I did not hear anything.'

Him: 'How odd!'

"After recalling what had happened, it occurred to us that right before my friend leaped to the ground, I had stomped on a piece of cardboard on the floor. What a funny story!

"Electricity cuts: How do we charge the camera batteries? How do we shoot indoor scenes? At night, everyone walks around with flashlights powered by small batteries... You could collide into a building of ten floors before seeing it through a Bolex camera, the best device for electricity cuts. The spring mechanism can sustain the camera (we discovered this in 1969 in Jordan, specifically at the fedayee bases where we sometimes spent more than two days). However, we found ourselves in need of a quiet camera that works synchronously with the audio recorder. What should we do? A couple of ideas came to mind, for example, to generate electricity using a hand-held generator by taking turns rotating it. But where could we locate such a device? Design it ourselves? Let's start. But where do we get the raw materials for production? Before long, Fatah imported generators operating on fuel. The problem was solved with a small and annoying generator that produced electricity for all seven departments of the Unified Information building. A single, low wattage lightbulb for each department.

"When we were brave enough to light a second bulb, the electricity cut for everyone.... Our brothers looked for a suitable place to put the generator, and they settled on a small space near the Palestinian Cinema Institution office.

Someone says, 'What did you say? Raise your voice!'

Another one says, '... I can't hear anything... raise your voice.'

"Because of the generator's noise, we joked about our new slogan: Darkness is better than light. With the electricity generator we were able to charge our batteries and filming was re-energized.

"Water was also cut off. The water interruption created captivating cinematic scenes, especially for color film: the colorful plastic buckets and bowls and people waiting to fill up gallons of water to be used for drinking and preparing food. Eventually, the scenes of people carrying their plastic water gallons, empty or full, became a regular occurrence, just like scenes of cigarette smoking. Some would carry buckets on their heads or by hand, others designed small carts for transportation. The photography department of the institute needed a lot of water, as developing film and printing photos required relatively large amounts. There were lots of films, but water was scarce. Once, we were forced to develop photos by immersing them in the fixing substance alone.

"During the days of the siege, getting bread, meat and vegetables became difficult...We ate canned goods ... canned goods. Nothing but canned goods. The filmmakers commented, 'If the cameras shake in our hands, we are not to blame.'"

The Biggest Burden on the Cinematographers

The militant filmmaker Omar Al-Mukhtar (Abdelhafeth Al-Asmar)[18] gave an interview just a few days before the Israeli invasion of Southern Lebanon. Omar and his colleague Mutee' (Ibrahim Naser) were martyred while covering the events on the first day of the invasion on March 15, 1978.

In the interview, Omar said: "At the Palestinian Cinema Institution, where we work collectively, we initially faced challenging difficulties,

---

[18] "We Are Originally Fighters," interview with the cinematographer Omar Al-Mukhtar, *Palestinian Image* magazine, First issue, November (Beirut: Palestinian Cinema Institution, 1978), p. 9–10. It is unclear who gave this interview as the writers often did not identify themselves by name.

especially when we filmed among our people who were very sensitive about the camera (perhaps because of previous experiences with foreign photographers who focused on capturing their suffering). However, our continued presence with the people and cohabitation amongst them contributed to changing this image. The sensitivities slowly eased away especially when we showed our first film in the camps. In our experience, filming the militants was much easier, because we were originally militants, and honestly we found no difficulty working in their midst."

He elaborated: "In reality, the cinematographers bore the heaviest burden of the work. Often, the cinematographer went alone or with one assistant to cover the events, because it was difficult to send an entire team during the war in Lebanon. A year after the start of the war, we formed groups consisting of a director, cinematographer, sound recorder, and photographer with the aim of producing a film. Often, we went as a group but no one except the cinematographer was able to reach the specific location. Our experience during the war was the most dangerous but also the most important for us.

"We covered the events we could reach, but the difficulties were often insurmountable. Sometimes, we were not able to film in the presence of those injured. Other times, militants did not tolerate the camera in their midst. One time, the militants captured the camera and destroyed it. Some of them were considerate, offering us help and guidance in traversing the battlefield, as well as securing protection for us. We realized that no matter how many filmmakers were on the ground, we were only able to cover a limited number of events, and a range of situations was not documented.

"The filming happened under difficult circumstances. During many days we were at the mercy of death. We would cross a street, and seconds afterwards someone would be killed by a sniper. When we were forced to cross a route controlled by a sniper, we waited two hours to traverse a 10-meter street.

"We tried covering all aspects of the war: the battles, crisis of food and water, garbage piled up in the streets, posters of martyrs. There was no designated time for work, we stayed alert night and day. When one filmmaker rested, another replaced him."

When asked whether he would help the injured, he responded: "There were always people taking care of the injured. I was never exposed to this situation, but in principle, the human is more important than the image. Human life is more important than photography. One could save the injured then photograph them. We do not photograph important events to respond to demands for high-speed newsgathering. We photograph as part of the revolution, and we cannot capitalize on people's pain. Our work is humanistic more than it is journalistic. We look for the truth, not for the news as such. Our primary concern is to present the news in all its human facets."

Cinematographer Samir Nimr Adds His Perspective[19]

"At the beginning, there were three people working at the PCI. We were joined by Lebanese friends who felt the importance of the situation and its dangers. They were photographers, filmmakers, critics and intellectuals. The aim of my presence at the PCI is to document and make films. These films could be about the resistance in Southern Lebanon against any form of Zionist military aggression, or in the camps, or in any place inhabited by the resistance. This was my role. The fighter's role is to deter attacks by the revolution's enemies. My role is to document, using image and sound, the struggle of the revolution and the people. I am a part of a whole. Like the fighter, the nurse, the doctor, and the person in charge of supplies or ammunition storage."

Samir was a very lively character. He directed a large number of films, the most important of which are *Kufrshuba* and *The Fifth War*, co-directed by German filmmaker Monica Maurer. The famous British actress Vanessa Redgrave[20] volunteered to play a major role in the film, in commemoration of the martyred filmmakers Mutee' and Omar who had worked with her on the production of *The Palestinian* in 1977.

BIBLIOGRAPHY

Abu Ali, Mustafa. "Shaheed al-Sinima al-Nidaliyah" ["The Martyr of the Militant Cinema"]. *Al-Surah al-Filastiniyah [Palestinian Image]*, First issue, November 1978, Beirut: Muassaset al-Sinima al-Filastiniyah p. 16-17.

Abu Ali, Mustafa. "Laqatat min al-Tajribah al-Sinima'iyah fi al-Harab al-Lubnaniyah (1975-1976)" ["Snapshots of the Cinematic Experience During

[19] Interview with Samir Nimr by Walid Chmait in *Palestine in Cinema*, 2nd ed. (Ramallah: Palestinian Ministry of Culture, 2006), p. 229.

[20] British actress Vanessa Redgrave started her career in theatre in Britain, then went on to act in several Hollywood films, winning the Oscar for Best Actress in the 1978 film *Julia*. She is also a political activist and a member of the British Worker's Revolutionary Party, and produced a documentary *The Palestinian* (1977), with the cooperation of the PCI.

the Lebanese War (1975-1976)". *Al-Surah al-Filastiniyah [Palestinian Image]*, First issue, November 1978, Beirut: Muassaset al-Sinima al-Filastiniyah, p. 15-19.

Abu Ali, Mustafa. "Hani ka Musawer" ["Hani as Cinematographer"]. *Al-Surah al-Filastiniyah [Palestinian Image]*, Second issue, March 1979, Beirut: Muassaset al-Sinima al-Filastiniyah, p. 9-14.

Abu Ghanimeh, Hassan. *Filastin wa-al'Ayn al-Sinima'I [Palestine and the Cinematic Eye]*. Damascus: Ittihad al-Kuttab al-'Arab, 1981.

Chmait, Walid and Guy Hennebelle, eds. *Filastin fi al-Sinima [Palestine in Cinema]*, 2nd ed. Ramallah: Wizarat al-Thaqafah al-Filastiniyah, al-Hay'ah al-'Ammah al-Filastiniyah lil Kitab, 2006.

"Nihnu fi al-Asl Muqatilun" ["We Are Originally Militants"], interview with cinematographer Omar Al-Mukhtar, *Al-Surah al-Filastiniyah [Palestinian Image]*. First issue, 1978, Beirut: Muassaset al-Sinima al-Filastiniyah, p. 9-10. (Author NA)

CHAPTER 6

Accelerated Development at the Institute

The pace of the development of the Palestine Film Unit picked up in the second half of the 1970s as the unit transformed into the Palestinian Cinema Institution. A notable improvement in the equipment and expansion of the staff followed. New personnel working in various artistic capacities joined, from photographers to cinematographers to sound engineers, in addition to administrative staff working on archiving, financing, and distribution. Among the new personnel, I recall these people:

Omar Al-Rashidi, Marwan Salameh, Khalil Sa'adeh, Mohammad Awad, Musa Maragha, Muwafaq Barakat: Cinematographers
Sufyan Al-Ramahi: Filmmaker
Janin Albina: Translator
Shaher Al-Soumi, Edward Al Qash: Sound engineers
Fahd Alawi, Intisar: Management
Amneh Naser: Secretary
Samirah Darbaj, Subheyieh Dabajeh: Archive assistants
Hind Jawharieh: Distribution
Jamal Nassar: Videographer
Jihad Abu Najeeleh, Mohammad Al-Rawwas, and others: Photographers

Many of these young men and women were sent to training courses or on scholarships to specialize in the technical skills of photography,

K. Habashneh, *Knights of Cinema*, Palgrave Studies in Arab Cinema, https://doi.org/10.1007/978-3-031-18858-9_6

cinematography, sound recording and sound technology that were needed at the institute between 1976 and 1980. From the photography team, I recall Ibrahim Al-Msadar and Yousef Qutob were sent to East Germany. Also sent to Germany at different times were Omar Al-Rashidi, Khalil Sa'adeh, Shaher Al-Soumi, Marwan Salameh, Musa Maragha, and Muwafaq Barakat.

Some of them returned to work at the PCI. Omar Al-Rashidi returned to the PCI after an intensive course in cinematography following the martyrdom of Mutee' and Omar. Shaher Al-Soumi returned to work as a sound engineer. Khalil Sa'adeh returned to work as a cinematographer and remained with the PCI until after the siege of Beirut and the PLO's departure to Tunis. Ibrahim Al-Msadar and Yousef Qutob returned to work at the institute even though the photography department of the PCI was managed separately after Mutee's martyrdom.

Some of those who joined the PCI also worked, at different stages, at the PLO Chairman's Office, including Janin Albina, Jamal Nassar, and Mohammad Al-Rawwas. During the siege of Beirut and the Tunis period, Khalil Sa'adeh worked between both offices, and Omar Al-Rashidi dedicated his entire time to the PLO Chairman's Office toward the end of the Tunis period.

Some of those who were sent abroad for training did not return for personal circumstances or because of the Israeli siege on Beirut in 1982 and the events that followed.

During my work on the book, I contacted most of the filmmakers of the PFU/PCI to verify dates and information about their work and the work of their colleagues. Those I interviewed include Mahmoud Nofal, Yousef Qutub, Omar Al-Rashidi, Shaher Al-Soumi, and Khalil Sa'adeh.

When I spoke with Khalil Sa'adeh, he interrupted me before the end of the interview to say (notes in parentheses below are mine):

"A moment before we finish, Um Ammar (as everyone called me at the PCI): I want to tell you about an incident that you must promise to publish. Mustafa Abu Ali is a very important director and truly the founder of revolutionary cinema. In my opinion, this militant has not received due attention and has been wronged because he was very humble. I want to tell you about an incident I witnessed myself when Youssef Shaheen filmed an interview with Abu Ammar, and Mustafa was present. Abu Ammar [Yasser Arafat] asked Youssef to make a film about Palestine. He quickly responded: 'You have an important director like Mustafa, and you want me to make a film about Palestine. Can I possibly express more about Palestine than Mustafa?'

"Another incident I witnessed that I'll never forget is when I came back from a training workshop in Germany. I asked Mustafa, who was in charge of the PCI, to raise my compensation (compensation was 'salary' in Fatah's dictionary). When I checked in with finance about my compensation, I discovered that it had become 1164 Lebanese Lira, which was more than the 1000 Lira compensation that Mustafa received. I truly felt embarrassed. When I confronted Mustafa about the issue, he said, 'My job as the manager is to appreciate the efforts of those working at the institute, not to evaluate my own work.' Later, I learned that everyone who worked at the PCI in the last years received more compensation than Mustafa."[1]

Establishing the Archive of Palestinian Cinema

Since the establishment of the photography department at Fatah's Information Office, the group's effort was increasingly directed to documenting events and transmitting an image of the Palestinian Revolution to the world. With the beginnings of the Palestine Film Unit until the mid-1970s, a huge amount of film footage was accumulated. The available labor and resources did not allow the PFU to do anything more than label the boxes of film reel.

The Palestinian Cinema Institution [PCI] continued documenting all events that had to do with the revolution and the Palestinian people, compiling the richest photography and film archive of the Palestinian Revolution's political and military activities, and public activities in the camps and the other places where Palestinians lived.

Over time, retrieving specific shots needed for films became increasingly difficult. An archival and classification system became necessary to provide the appropriate conditions to preserve the film reels and important cinematic documents.

My effort to organize and archive films began as soon as I was free to dedicate time to the PCI in 1974 and especially after receiving an editing machine gifted to the unit by an ally state. I can't recall whether it was the Soviet Union or Libya.

During the escalation of the war in Beirut and the siege of Tal Al-Za'atar, continuous bombardment caused the disruption of many aspects of everyday life like water, electricity, and mobility, and many members spent most of their time at the PCI office. In this, I found the opportunity to organize

[1] From an informal conversation I had with Khalil Sa'adeh in 2019.

the material after completing a course on archiving various media at the Planning Center [one of the centers of the PLO concerned with planning and programming different activities to develop the work of PLO institutions] in preparation for the work. I dove into watching and organizing all the accumulated film reels, which took several months and led to the establishment of the department of the archive and cinematheque. The filmed material was organized according to date, subject, event, theme, or personality. This last category included leaders of the PLO from different organizations like George Habash, high-ranking military officers like Abu Jihad (Khalil Al Wazir), distinguished political and intellectual cadres like Mahmoud Darwish, the head of the PLO office in France Ezzedine Qalaq, and other historical figures in the national struggle. The newly filmed footage directly entered the new classification system, which helped in retrieving things.

Two new staff members were hired as assistants to receive the new footage. They reviewed and catalogued all the footage content before categorizing it under my supervision. Among the material purchased for the archive was a specialized cabinet that stored information about the film reels on non-perishable material. The archive room was also furnished with an air-conditioning unit to preserve the material at an appropriate temperature, and a plan was implemented to film additional events and interviews with the leaders and the distinguished cadres for the purpose of documentation and archiving. After the arrangement of the archive, I had the time to think about the script for the first film I directed, *Children Without Childhood*, which was made in response to the International Declaration of Child Rights, issued by the UN in 1979.

In 1976, the PCI grew to include a third department of archiving and cinematheque (Film Library), with a collection of around ninety films, among them Palestinian films and films produced by revolutionary cinema groups around the Palestinian cause or other revolutions and popular liberation movements around the world, from Cuba, Vietnam, China, the Soviet Union, and cinema of the third world in general.

When the PCI needed to buy film footage of Palestine shot at the beginning of the twentieth century from one of the foreign news agencies to use in a documentary film, we were surprised by the exorbitant amount requested at the time, especially as we had very limited resources. The agency asked for 22 pounds sterling for every foot (30 cm) of historic footage. In addition to the historic and national value of the documents we have, this incident drew our attention to the financial value, and the critical importance of preserving the treasures we have for our people.

After the development of the archive department, we established a form for requesting film footage from the archive. It included questions about the requested topic, duration or length of material, and the purpose of use. A signature at the end confirmed a pledge to use the material for purposes that align and do not contradict with the mission of Palestinian cinema.

In July 1981, Israel bombarded, for the first time, the Fakahani district in Beirut. We began to feel that the archive was in real danger.

In addition to its value and importance, the archive had cost us several martyred filmmakers, which made its defense a sacred imperative for us. We started thinking about moving the archive and film library from the office of the PCI, located in the area of the Arab Union alongside the majority of offices and headquarters of the Palestinian resistance. We initially thought of making a copy (dupe negatives) of the archive and preserving it safely abroad, in an ally state. After considering the costs, we realized that creating a duplicate of each film was not feasible. We switched to considering an underground storage facility. We rented a large basement in a building in Al-Hamra district and prepared it with the necessary ventilation system that would allow for climate-controlled temperature and humidity required for preserving film material. We hid the intentions of renting the storage space and quickly moved the archive there.

PALESTINE FILM UNIT/PALESTINIAN CINEMA INSTITUTION COLLABORATIONS

From the beginning of the 1970s, the PFU/PCI quickly evolved to become a center that attracted Arab and international filmmakers with whom they shared a mutual collaboration and for whom they provided services. Among them, I recall the Third World Cinema filmmakers from Argentina who came in 1971, Algerian director Mohmmad Salim Riyad who made the film *We Will Return* in 1973, jointly produced by Algeria and Palestine; the Danish director Nils Vest who came in 1973 and made the film *An Oppressed People Is Always Right*, released in 1975; and the German director Manfred Foss who made *Al-Rashidiyyeh* in 1975, produced by Germany in collaboration with Palestine.

The Vincennes Cinema Group from France (Serge Le Péron, Guy Chapoullié, Jean Narboni) made the film *The Olive Tree in* 1975, in collaboration with the PCI, facilitated by the PLO office in France headed by the Palestinian intellectual Ezzedine Qalaq. Following Ezzedine's martyrdom, the group also made a film about his life and struggle in 1978 based on an interview I conducted with Ezzedine for the Archive in 1977.

Lebanese director Randa Chahal participated with the works of the PCI through conducting interviews with those injured and displaced from Tal Al-Za'atar in 1976. She also directed the film *Step by Step* about the Lebanese war, which was produced by the PCI.

British actress Vanessa Redgrave and British director Roy Battersby came to Beirut in coordination with the leadership of Fatah. They produced a film about the Palestinian revolution in Fatah entitled *The Palestinian* in collaboration with the PCI. This film caused Vanessa a lot of trouble with the Zionist lobby, and she was boycotted by film producers for several years.

Lebanese/Egyptian director Nabeeha Lutfi came to Beirut in the beginning of 1976 to make a film about the women of Tal Al-Za'atar camp in cooperation with the General Union of Palestinian Women before the siege of the camp. After filming a number of interviews with women from the camp, the siege from the isolationist forces (the popular name for the Lebanese right-wing forces) started and intensified, and she was unable to finish filming inside the camp. She made the film *Because Roots Don't Die* at the end of 1977 about the struggles and sufferings of women in Tal Al-Za'atar before, during, and after the siege.

German director Monica Maurer came in 1978 on a solidarity visit with the Palestinian Red Crescent, and made some films on Palestinian issues, in collaboration with the PCI filmmakers, Samir Nimr and Abu Thareef. They completed a number of films co-directed with Samir Nimr. Among the most important are *Children of Palestine* and *The Fifth War*, both in 1978.

THE PALESTINIAN CINEMA INSTITUTION ATTRACTS PALESTINIAN AND ARAB FILMMAKERS

The Palestinian director **Ghaleb Sha'ath** came to the institute in 1975. He was born in Jerusalem in 1934 and fled with his family in 1948 to Egypt. There, he completed his secondary education, and received a diploma in engineering in Vienna in 1964, and a diploma in directing from the Vienna Cinema Institute in 1967. Upon graduating, he returned to Egypt, where he worked in Egyptian cinema. He directed the film *Shadows on the Other Side* (1974) with the New Cinema Group in Egypt.

Ghaleb found that PCI work was limited to documentary, and he wanted to continue his work on narrative films as he had done in Egypt. He joined SAMED,[2] hoping to direct feature narrative films. Unfortunately, his dream of making fiction films was not realized, but he directed three documentaries that were widely celebrated and distributed. They include *The Key* (1976), *Land Day* (1977), and *Olive Branch* (1978).

Lebanese film director **Jean Chamoun** was born in 1942 in the village of Sareen in the Beqa'a Valley in Lebanon. He studied theater at the Art Institute of Lebanese University and participated in several notable productions in the history of Lebanese theater including the plays *Al-Majdaloun, I am a Voter*, and *Caligula*, among others. In 1970, he went to France and received a master's degree in cinema from Paris 8 University Vincennes Saint-Denis, and a diploma in directing from the Luis Meilleur Institute in Paris. Upon his return in 1974, he worked in Lebanese television, then went on to prepare and host a satirical program about the events of the Lebanese war, entitled *We Are Still Alive, Praise Be to God* (*Baidna Taybeen, oul Allah*), with Ziad Al-Rahbani in 1975.

At the end of 1975 and beginning of 1976, Chamoun joined the PCI. He started participating in the works of the institution by filming events of the war after the incident at Ain Al-Rummaneh on April 13, 1975, where bullets were fired on a bus approaching from Tal Al-Za'atar refugee camp, killing more than twenty-six people.

In 1977, Chamoun participated in directing the film *Tal Al-Za'atar* with Mustafa Abu Ali and Pino Adriano, a journalist from the Italian Communist Party.

In 1980, Chamoun participated in the International Youth Festival in Cuba, as part of the Palestinian delegation representing the PCI. He produced a film about the festival entitled *Hymn of Liberty*. He also recorded

---

[2] SAMED is a political and economic organization that developed from the Palestine Martyrs and Prisoners Families Society which was established by Al-'Asifah, the military wing of Fatah. In the mid-1970s the society established factories that manufactured things like clothing, furniture, and shoes. After the development of the war in Lebanon when Beirut became split into the East and West side with escalated violence between these two sides, it was difficult for those working in cinema in West Beirut to continue their work at Studio Ba'albak, which was located in Sin Al-Fil in East Beirut. For this reason, SAMED built Studio Al-Sakhra for editing, which included a laboratory for film development and printing.

footage of the siege of Beirut in 1982 in collaboration with the Palestinian filmmaker Mai Masri who had recently arrived in Beirut to participate in Palestinian cinema. The footage was used in a film directed by Jean entitled *Under the Rubble*. This was the first of many collaborations by both filmmakers, who would later realize many jointly produced films.

WORKING ON *TAL AL-ZA'ATAR*[3] DURING THE WAR

Mustafa Abu Ali recalls:

"We are now in mid-1976 ... the airport is shut ... we have 15,000 meters of footage in color, negative, and reversal, and no place in Beirut to develop it.

"Some footage has been in boxes for three and a half months. Anxiety spreads everywhere. This material will definitely be damaged if it isn't quickly developed. Europe is the solution. But we don't have enough funds to develop the material there.

"What about co-production? I contact various entities, saying, 'We have 15,000 meters about the war, and we need someone to work with us on a co-production.'

"Finally, we contact the Italian Communist Party, through a connection from our brother Majed Abu Sharar, the head of the Unified Information Office... We have Agfachrome, Ektachrome, and Eastman color film.... Can we develop them in Italy? There is nothing we can't develop in Italy. This was the answer. One hundred and fifty kilograms of film will be transported from Saida to Cyprus by ship. The ship is delayed until tomorrow because of the weather, but the weather is good; it looks like the delay was for security reasons. Tomorrow, we will board small boats to get to the ship. The next day we take these boats to board a ship. Now we are in the sea with all of our cargo.

"Suddenly, a voice calls out, 'Get inside, get inside. The Israelis are here.' I look around... On the horizon there is a small grey dot. It slowly grows and as it approaches it appears to be a military boat guarded by manned machine guns ready to fire. A Cypriot sailor waves with his hands

---

[3] *Tal Al-Za'atar*, was a coproduction between the Palestinian Cinema Institution and Unitelefilm, which was affiliated with the Italian Communist Party. The film revolves around the experiences of the people and the political leadership in the camp during the siege imposed by the Isolationist forces (Lebanese Kata'ib Party and National Liberal Party). The siege and the resistance lasted more than fifty days.

to the soldiers, they don't respond. The military boat circles our ship twice. Thoughts of fear and concern over losing the films fill my mind. We whisper aboard the ship. It would be a disaster if they come and search us!! But finally, they leave from where they emerged. I feel humiliation and resentment. It was truly a shameful incident. A small civilian ship in the Mediterranean Sea is confronted by a military boat armed with soldiers ready to fire, contempt emanating from them. They can do anything they want to us. They had previously detained the Lebanese militant (Nahla Chahal), and they took her and her friend with them to Israel for no reason. What prevents them from detaining us and taking our films?

"After 24 hours, we finally arrive in Cyprus. I wait a week before I secure a seat on a plane headed to Rome. At the airport, the films are seized for a week, and I wait as if I were standing on a flame. The films will be damaged if they are not developed. Finally, I receive an important piece of information 'The Agfachrome films can't be developed in Rome. What can we do?' Let's go… to France… Two weeks later, I take the films and head to the film lab in Paris with the help of Unicité[4] and in coordination with Unitelefilm. In Rome, there are specialized organizations, but instead of the films returning to Rome to start work on the film *Tal Al-Za'atar*, they are delayed for three months at Unicité despite daily communications. The work is delayed for silly reasons outside the scope of discussion here, and some material also went missing in this period.

"*Tal Al-Za'atar* was released after an immense amount of effort and stress that plagued the co-production process. Work on this film was not just challenging, but a true translation of the meaning of solidarity between revolutionary forces. I can say, confidently that we have succeeded in the test, despite the immense difficulties Jean and I experienced.

"After *Tal Al-Za'atar* was complete, we had 10,000 meters of unused film roll remaining, in addition to the black and white film. We planned to make a film about the Lebanese War, highlighting historical, social and political dimensions, and placing Lebanon within the framework of struggles in the Arab world and the Middle East."[5]

---

[4] Unicité, a French company for film production and distribution.
[5] Mustafa Abu Ali, "Snapshots of the Cinematic Experience During the Lebanese War (1975–1976)", in *Palestinian Image* magazine, First Issue November (Beirut: Palestinian Cinema Institution, 1978), p. 19.

Letter from Mustafa as He Worked on Tal Al-Zaʿatar[6]

Khadijah...

I miss you...

Jean Abu Khalil[7] is here, so is Rasmy. Their presence eases the situation, but I still feel intense longing for you. How is Ammar? I received your letter, and with it the beautiful picture of the two of you. I will definitely bring back what he asked for....

The work: Jean's presence here has had a very positive effect, because the co-production was about to collapse. Upon his arrival, the situation has improved. The reason for the tension, I discovered, was that the students interpreting for me were mistranslating which led to a huge miscommunication between me and the collaborators. Isn't that weird? When Jean arrived, his command of French made it easy to communicate with them and things have moved on quickly. We discovered together that the problem was a simple misunderstanding. We all humored the situation and laughed it off together. We regained the trust that had been lost in mistranslation.

The situation has confirmed the importance of Jean's continued presence in Rome, as I have felt since my arrival a need to have someone with me. And Jean seems to be best in this case.

Tal Al-Zaʿatar, as I had mentioned to you, no longer interests the party here. Because one of my goals is to follow through with this co-production, I have tolerated a lot, especially in delays to the start of the work. My conviction has been that we need to extend to Europe, even if it comes with some sacrifice. This is useful to us politically and cinematically, especially in terms of distribution.

Today, Unitelefilm's contribution to the film decreased from 50 percent to 25 percent, and we must pay the equivalent of 7 million Italian pounds to complete the work, and an additional 3 million if we want to own the material of the Beirut film, to compensate for the development of the footage (Figs. 6.1 and 6.2).

May 17, 1977

---

[6] The original letter, and other correspondence with Mustafa about work on *Tal Al-Zaʿatar*, are reproduced in Appendix B.

[7] This was a nickname for Jean Chamoun.

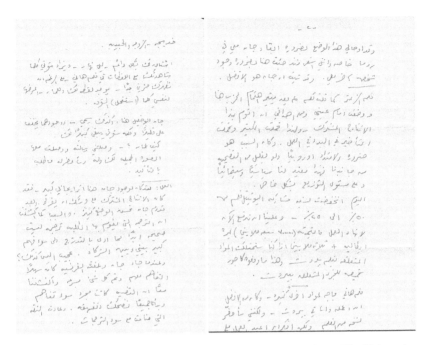

Figs. 6.1 and 6.2 Original letter in Arabic from Mustafa to Khadijeh as he worked on *Tal Al-Za'atar*

Screenings Organized by the Film Library (Cinematheque)

As the PFU/PCI expanded its networks, we accumulated a number of militant films about Palestine and other ally movements around the world, such as films about the popular revolutions and liberation movements of Vietnam, Cambodia, China, Soviet Union, Cuba, and Nicaragua, among other places. There were about ninety films at the archive and film library. This encouraged the Unified Information Office to offer its ground floor as a screening space for employees of the office and other revolutionary organizations interested in attending. Following the screenings, a report was produced describing the film and the conversations that ensued around it. The screenings often took place on Thursday evenings. However, they did not happen regularly because of the conditions of the war and were often postponed or stopped for a period of time.

Training Sessions to Develop Skills of New Personnel

The screening room was also used to conduct training sessions on filming, sound recording, and directing, to develop the skills of the new personnel of the PCI. This was done until grants and scholarships became available for specialized training at institutes in allied countries.

Several young men from Yemen and Eritrea also graduated from these workshops and received training in filmmaking alongside employees of the PCI (Figs. 6.3, 6.4, 6.5, 6.6 and 6.7).

More Palestinian and Arab filmmakers Join the PCI

After Hani Jawharieh's martyrdom in 1976 and the empty space left by the absence of the two original founders of the unit, Mustafa was increasingly in need of support to enrich and grow the PCI. Jean Chamoun arrived at the right time in the middle of 1976. A number of other people who were instrumental in their contributions joined.

Fig. 6.3   The artist Mustafa Al-Hallaj conducts a training session in the screening room at the PCI, 1978

Fig. 6.4 Other view of artist Mustafa Al-Hallaj in a training session in the screening room at the PCI, 1978

Fig. 6.5 German director Manfred Foss at the PCI in a film training workshop alongside Mutee', Ghaleb Sha'ath, Jamal Nassar, Sulafa Jadallah, as well as a friend and assistant of Foss, late 1977

Fig. 6.6 Palestinian director Ghaleb Sha'ath translates for Manfred Foss. On the left is Samir Nimr and the trainees from Yemen and Eritrea, late 1977

هورس شتوم مع يوسف القطب في لبنان 1981

Fig. 6.7 German news agency photographer Horst Schtom with Palestinian photographer Yousef Qutob, 1981

Adnan Madanat, the Jordanian filmmaker and critic joined the PCI in late 1976. Born in Jordan in 1946, he grew up and completed his secondary studies in Damascus, where his family lived and his father worked. He studied cinema and television journalism in Moscow. Upon graduation, he returned to Damascus and worked at the General Cinema Organization in 1972, where he directed the film *Melody for Several Seasons.* In 1976, he moved to Beirut and worked with the DFLP. While there, he directed the film *News About Tal Al-Za'atar* which has been lost. After that he joined the PCI.

Madanat recalls joining the PCI:[8]

> Mustafa called me after Hani Jawharieh was martyred and asked me to work with him at the PCI because they lacked personnel. I joined the PCI, and the Lebanese director Jean Chamoun had joined before me. We established a committee amongst ourselves to lay down a work plan for developing the institute. It included delineating roles for personnel at the institute, establishing a salary ladder and a system of compensation that corresponds with the intensity of the work. We agreed to establish yearly budget plans for production and distribution. We met with the head of the Unified Information Office, Majed Abu Sharar, who was excited about the expansion. However, a long time passed, and the plan was not accomplished.

After that, Adnan was free to work on his film *Palestinian Visions* in 1977, produced by the PCI. After the release of the first issue of the *Palestinian Image* magazine, he joined its editorial board, which he went on to lead as it expanded to include a number of filmmakers, critics, and artists.

Fouad Zantout, a Lebanese editor, and film director, edited a large number of the PCI's films and newsreels from the beginning of the 1970s. He joined the PCI full time at the end of 1977.

Najah Kayyouf, a Lebanese editor, worked as a freelancer on most of the PCI's films from the beginning of the 1970s until the early 1980s.

Yahya Barakat, a Palestinian director, arrived from Cairo upon graduating from the Higher Institute of Cinema, and joined the PCI in 1978. In 1981, he was nominated to make a film about the life of Palestinian poet Abu Salma. The project, however, was postponed because of special circumstances related to financing. He later continued to work on the film with the Culture and Information Department of the PLO in late 1982.

[8] Information obtained in an informal conversation with Adnan Madanat, 2019.

Hikmat Daoud, an Iraqi film director, joined the PCI in 1980 after working with the cinema committee of the DFLP. In 1981, after the assassination of the head of the Unified Information Office, Majed Abu Sharar, Hikmat took over. He directed a film about Abu Sharar and continued to work with the department of media and culture in Damascus after the PLO and its institutions left Beirut. The film *Forever in Our Memory* was released in 1982.

Mohammad Tawfiq, an Iraqi film director, joined the institute in 1980 after working with the cinema committee of the DFLP. He directed the film *The Child and the Toy,* which was not completed until after 1982. The film was released in Tunis in 1983.

Janeen Tawfiq 'Awwad, an Iraqi editor, joined the PCI at the beginning of the 1980s. She worked on the number of films with the PCI and continued her contribution in Tunis.

Eman Khadir, an Iraqi filmmaker, joined the PCI in 1981.

Mohammad Al-Sawalmeh, a Palestinian director, graduated from the Cinema Institute in Moscow. He arrived toward the end of 1981 and did not manage to direct any films before the siege of Beirut. In Tunis, he directed several films including *The Longest Day* in 1983 which revolved around the catastrophe of the Shatila massacre, and *Last Fifteen Minutes* in 1988 which was about the first Palestinian intifada in 1987.

THE *PALESTINIAN IMAGE* MAGAZINE

Throughout the PFU/PCI's journey, there were many discussions and attempts to define revolutionary and militant cinema, or alternative cinema, as some called it. The concept of Palestinian cinema was misunderstood by some critics who saw it as propaganda for Palestinian organizations; others went so far as to doubt the existence of Palestinian cinema. This necessitated a space for communicating and reflecting on the general meaning and direction of cinema, with a specific focus on militant and revolutionary cinema. This required the PCI to issue the first edition of the *Palestinian Image* magazine, which was published in November 1978. A steering committee for the magazine was organized to include Palestinian and Arab filmmakers and artists working in the space of revolutionary cinema. The committee included Jordanian director and critic Adnan Madanat and Lebanese director Jean Chamoun upon the publication of the second edition in March 1979. Later, the committee expanded to include Jordanian artist Muna Saudi, Palestinian artist Mustafa Al-Hallaj,

Iraqi director Qais Al-Zubaidi, and Palestinian director Ghalib Sha'ath. Mustafa Abu Ali was the supervisor, and Adnan Madanat was the editor-in-chief. Four issues of the magazine were published, the last in November 1979.

Although Mustafa used to write the opening article of each issue, the magazine covered many cinematic issues and was open to all filmmakers, critics, intellectuals, and enthusiasts. Some examples include "On the Zionist Cinema" by Jean Chamoun about the film *We Are Arab Jews in Israel*; "The Search for a Popular Cinema" by the Bolivian film director Jorge Sanjines, originally published in the Cuban magazine *Tricontinental*, no. 92,1974, which I translated from English; "Israel, Palestine, What Cinema Can Do" by Adnan Madanat; "The Beginning: Was a Picture" by Mustafa Al Halaj; "Zionist Cinema and the Culture of Oppression and Settlement" by Israeli writer Alan Zaif, translated from American magazine *Cineaste* by Iraqi writer Sadiq Al Sayegh,; "Primary Planning on the Meaning of Cinema" by Qais Al Zubaidi; and "Panel on Revolution and Culture" by Adnan Madanat.

THE MARTYRDOM OF MUTEE' AND OMAR[9]

Mutee' (Ibrahim Naser) and Omar (Abdelhafeth Al-Asmar) were martyred on March 15, 1978, during the Israeli invasion and bombardment of Southern Lebanon, according to Yousef Qutob and Abu Thareef (Tawfiq Khalil), both of whom accompanied the team (Fig. 6.8).

The four filmmakers and two photographers headed to Southern Lebanon to film the Israeli bombardment on March 14, 1978. Once they reached the area of Saff Al-Hawa to document the destruction, they split up into two groups after being fired upon by an Israeli tank. Ibrahim Al-Msadar, Yousef Qutob, and Abu Thareef headed toward the upper area, while Ibrahim Naser, Abdelhafeth Al-Asmar, and Ramzi Al-Rassi[10] went toward the lower area. The first group disappeared behind the mountain and were no longer immediate targets.

---

[9] Based on a report in commemoration of the martyred filmmakers Ibrahim Naser and Abdelhafeth Al-Asmar, prepared by journalist Zulfa Shahrour for the Palestine News Agency—Wafa, March 2018.

[10] Ramzi Al-Rassi is a Lebanese photographer who studied in the UK, worked for a news agency, and was a friend to the PCI.

Fig. 6.8   The filmmakers Mutee' and Omar, cameras ready in hand

The following account was recently obtained from Ramzi Al-Rassi, who would be arrested by the Israelis and released months later, in 1978:

Ramzi Al-Rassi's Story of Mutee' and Omar's Last Days[11]

Saff Al Hawa, Bint Jubail, 1978

"On the morning of March 15th, a film crew from the Palestinian Film Institution was about to leave for South Lebanon, and I asked if I could join them. Reports already reached Beirut describing heroic resistance to the Israeli advance. Hence, enthusiasm amongst the team was euphoric.

"We were five in the car: I sat with two photographers in the back seat. In the front, sat the two senior cameramen: Omar driving and Mutee' next to him holding the 16 mm Beaulieu camera on his lap, very much like a warrior on his way to battle. Omar and Mutee' were highly experienced cameramen boasting an impressive history of documenting Palestinian action. They considered their work as a mission to serve the cause. We

[11] Ramzi Al-Rassi's account was written in a personal letter to Khadijeh Habashneh, January 3, 2022.

headed south along the coastal road, aiming to reach the town of Bint Jubail, where fierce clashes were reported to have taken place. I suggested that we make inquiries about the Israeli advance and establish our safe routes accordingly. However, my colleagues in the car did not see the need to make such inquiries.

"We arrived at Saff Al Hawa, an intersection of roads leading to different directions. We saw two parked cars with people standing on the edge of the road. Some of them were holding still cameras and looking at the town of Bint Jubail, which was within a walking distance. We assumed that they were journalists from Beirut, so we disembarked and joined them.

"Mutee' held the camera on his shoulder, panned across the town through its powerful zoom lens. He murmured the word 'tank' (which he saw through the viewfinder). There was no time to react. A cascade of machine-gun bullets started falling on us, so we all scattered and ran. The sound of the machine gun was so loud, which implied that the source of fire was close by.

"I later found out that the journalists managed to reach their two cars and drive away. The two photographers who sat next to me, managed to run safely down the sloping road towards Tibneen. Omar, Mutee' (who was carrying the camera), and I ran to the other side of the intersection, away from the bullets. We climbed the hill and the bullets followed our footsteps, until we took shelter at the entrance of a small concrete structure. I learned later that the structure was one of many bunkers built by the Arab League in the early seventies to protect Lebanese civilians from Israeli shelling.

"A shell exploded in our midst. My right eye was badly injured and I could barely see with my left eye. Omar and Mutee' were lying some three meters away, badly injured with stomach wounds and amputated legs, so they couldn't move. They were, however, fully conscious, talking to me calmly and giving me instructions. The 16 mm camera was shattered to pieces next to them. I took off my white undershirt and waived it. I shouted in Arabic, English, and French that we were journalists and injured civilians. That was of course a wasted effort, because the Israelis had already seen us at Saff Al Hawa, and seen that we (and the other journalists from Beirut) were civilians, carrying cameras, not weapons. I couldn't do much to help Omar and Mutee'. They continued chatting calmly to each other and submitting to the will of God.

"I heard the sound of an approaching tank. I moved forward and waived my white t-shirt. When the tank was around ten meters away, a soldier stepped out from behind the tank and opened machine-gun fire. Omar and Mutee', who couldn't move because of their wounds, were lying on their backs and courageously faced the tank. They were hit in cold blood by criminal bursts of machine-gun fire that decimated their bodies from head all the way down.

"I ran down the stairs to the underground bunker. A hand grenade rolled down and exploded, followed by four more grenades which exploded, one at a time. I was injured in various places. I was asked to put my hands up and come out. When I reached the bottom of the stairs, a helmeted soldier opened fire. I was hit by a bullet in my waist, which thrust me on my back. The Israelis assumed that I was killed. I stayed put in the bunker for two nights, while the Israelis immediately set up a military camp just outside of it. Walking out was not an option.

"In the morning of the third day the Israelis left their positions outside the bunker. I climbed up the stairs and waved to civilians who were walking on the asphalt road to Tibneen, some thirty meters down the hill. I got to know later that those civilians were a film crew from the Tel Aviv office of the Visnews agency, who were filming for the BBC correspondent John Bierman. They filmed everything, including the moment when the Israelis grabbed me as I walked out of the bunker. I managed to say a few words to the camera - that we were civilians, came from Beirut, filming etc.

"I lost consciousness and was eventually taken to an Israeli hospital. I later discovered that the Visnews/BBC report filmed the bodies of Omar and Mutee', still lying at the other entrance. The report mentioned that they died from 'previously sustained wounds.' I was told later that the report was aired on the BBC and some 100 other subscriber channels around the world.

"Following the airing of the report, the Israelis admitted my presence to the International Committee of the Red Cross. In hospital, Harald De Gruneck, the head of the ICRC office in Tel Aviv visited me and told me that I was the 'only prisoner' in that war. He also told me that following the BBC report, some press associations in France and Switzerland were making queries about me and about the deaths of Omar and Mutee'. Three weeks, later the Israelis handed me over to ICRC, who drove me straight to Beirut" (Fig. 6.9).

Ramzi Al-Rassi

Fig. 6.9 Poster commemorating the martyrdom of Ibrahim Naser (Mutee') and Abdelhafeth Al-Asmar (Omar)

FRIENDS OF THE PALESTINIAN CINEMA INSTITUTION

The work of the PCI was significantly enhanced by the contribution of volunteer efforts by many Arab and European film critics and filmmakers. The following people were great friends of the PCI.

Ezzedine Qalaq was an intellectual militant and head of the Palestine office at the Arab League who later became the head of the PLO office in France and a political and Palestinian diplomat. He was very interested in arts and culture, and a friend of the Palestine Film Unit (PFU) since its early days in Beirut. He later played an important role in strengthening the PCI's relationship with progressive filmmakers in France and contributed to the *Palestinian Image* magazine with articles about Palestinian cinema at its inception. He also reviewed several films by French directors in an article entitled "Palestine Is Not a Phantom." He established a branch of the Palestinian Cinema Institution at the PLO office in France, where he had a special stamp that carried the name and the logo of the PCI France Office. He oversaw the connections between the PCI and French filmmakers and paid personal attention to distributing and screening Palestinian films.

Guy Hennebelle, **a French writer and film critic**, wrote about Palestinian cinema and visited the PCI twice in 1977 and 1978. He worked on preparing a number of books on Palestinian cinema, including one with the Tunisian film critic Khamis Khayyati and another with the Lebanese critic Walid Chmait, all of whom were friends of the PCI.

Taher Al-Cheriaa, founder of the Carthage Days of Cinema Festival in 1966, was among the first friends of the PCI from its early days. He was a member of the jury at the Damascus International Festival for Youth Cinema in April 1972, where he met Mustafa. After that, Al-Cheriaa visited the PFU in Beirut and then invited the PFU to attend the Carthage Days of Cinema Festival in October 1972.

Horst Schtom, a German photographer working for a German news agency, was a friend of Palestinian cinema. He came to Beirut several times in 1978 and 1980 to train photographers at the PCI.

Serge Le Péron, a French filmmaker, critic, and member of the editorial committee of the French magazine *Cahiers De Cinema*, contributed to the magazine with an article entitled *Palestinian Cinema Does Exist*. He also wrote reviews of several films produced by the PCI.

Guy Chapouillie and Jean Narboni, French filmmakers who were members of the Vincennes Group who visited the PCI in Beirut in 1975 and produced the films *The Olive Tree* (1975) and *Ezzedine Qalaq* (1978).

Samir Farid, a well-known Egyptian film critic, wrote about the experience of Palestinian revolutionary cinema and introduced the works of the PFU/PCI on several occasions where no representative was present. He also wrote about how Zionist cinema organizations sabotaged the work of the Palestinian revolution.

Abdelkarim Qabous, a Tunisian film critic, was a very active writer who introduced PFU/PCI at its first participation at the Carthage Film Festival in 1972.

Ezzedine Al-Manasrah, a Palestinian militant and a poet, conducted research on Zionist cinema and was a friend of the PFU/PCI. He wrote about Palestinian cinema and participated in the PCI's delegations to several international festivals.

Mustafa Al-Hallaj, a Palestinian fine artist, was a friend of the PFU since its inception. He participated in training the PCI's personnel. He later served on the editorial committee of the *Palestinian Image* magazine and supported the PCI with his works and writings.

Muna Saudi, a Jordanian fine artist and sculptor, was a longtime friend of the PFU. She oversaw a number of the PCI communiques and served on the editorial committee of the *Palestinian Image* magazine in the 1970s.

Jocelyne Saab, a Lebanese filmmaker, was a friend from the first beginnings of the PFU, with whom there was reciprocal cooperation on several projects during the 1970s.

Randa Chahal (also known as Randa Chahal Sabbagh), a Lebanese filmmaker, worked on interviewing refugees fleeing Tal Al-Za'atar and directed a film *Khutwa Khutwa* (*Step by Step*) that was co-produced with the PCI.

Ghassan Matar, a Palestinian actor, was the head of the Palestinian Artist's Union and a friend of the PCI. He participated in the works of the PCI and the delegations sent to international festivals.

Qais Al-Zubaidi, an Iraqi filmmaker, conducted trainings at the PCI starting in 1979 and served on the editorial committee of the *Palestinian Image* magazine.

Youssef Shaheen, the famous Egyptian filmmaker, came to Beirut to visit the Palestinian revolution and the PCI to learn about the Palestinian revolution.

Costa Gavras, the Greek-French filmmaker, came to Beirut to learn about the reality of the Palestinian people and their revolution while he worked on the film *Hanna K.* While in Beirut, he visited the PCI to learn about their work.

Mohammad Malas, the Syrian filmmaker, was a friend of the PCI. He engaged the institute in conversations around his film *Al Manam* (*The Dream*) in 1980, and the PCI-affiliated cinematographer Khalil Sa'adeh initially worked on his team. The film was delayed for financial reasons and was later made as a co-production between the Culture and Information department of the PLO and Maram for Cinema and Film Production, based in Damascus.

Additional Palestinian, Lebanese, and Arab Photographers and Filmmakers who Collaborated with the PCI

There are many other friends of the PCI whom I was unable to meet or get to know due to my traveling and dual engagement with cinema and the work of the General Union of Palestinian Women.

Mohammad 'Awwad, a photojournalist, was always ready to cover for the PCI when there was a lot of work or lack of personnel.

Ramzi Al-Rassi, a Lebanese photographer, worked with the PCI on various projects. Most importantly, he accompanied the PCI's team on March 15, 1978, to cover the Israeli invasion of Southern Lebanon, during which he witnessed the murders of the martyrs Mutee' and Omar.

Dr. Muna Al-Sabban, an Egyptian film editor, edited several films for the PCI including my first film *Children Without Childhood*.

Edward Al-Qash, a Lebanese militant, collaborated on many works with the PCI, in the capacities of sound recording and photographer.

Sabah Jabbour, a Lebanese film editor, worked on my film about women and the revolution, *Women of My Country*, which was lost at the beginning of the siege in 1982.

BIBLIOGRAPHY

Abu Ali, Mustafa. "Laqatat min al-Tajribah al-Sinima'iyah fi al-Harab al-Lubnaniyah (1975-1976)" ["Snapshots of the Cinematic Experience During the Lebanese War (1975-1976)". *Al-Surah al-Filastiniyah [Palestinian Image]*, First issue, November, 1978, Beirut: Muassaset al-Sinima al-Filastiniyah, p.19.

CHAPTER 7

The Israeli Invasion of Southern Lebanon and the Siege of Beirut

After the events of Tal Al-Za'atar in 1976 and the escalating tensions between the separatist powers (Lebanese Kataeb Party and National Liberal Party) and the Joint Lebanese-Palestinian Forces (a coalition of leftist Lebanese national forces headed by Kamal Jumblatt and allied with Yasser Arafat heading the PLO), those working in cinema were no longer able to go to East Beirut where Studio Ba'albak was located. As mentioned earlier, Studio Ba'albak's facilities were used for editing the PFU's first film *No to a Peaceful Solution* in 1969 and continued to serve as the production studio when the PFU/PCI expanded its work, while it also served other Palestinian and Lebanese groups working in cinema. Toward the end of 1976 and beginning of 1977, SAMED (Palestine Martyrs and prisoners Families Society) established Studio Al-Sakhra ("al-sakhra" meaning "the rock") for developing, printing, and editing films, in Bir Hassan, in the area known during the Lebanese Civil War as West Beirut.

On June 4, 1982, my friend, the Lebanese editor Sabah Jabbour, and I were editing my film *Women of My Country* at Studio Al-Sakhra. We worked until around 2 in the afternoon, when we discovered it was time for the children to return from school. At 4 o'clock that afternoon, as we were having a late lunch, we heard sounds of military jets and intense bombardment. I carried my young three-year-old child, and we all ran with our kids to the building's staircase.

© The Author(s), under exclusive license to Springer Nature Switzerland AG 2023
K. Habashneh, *Knights of Cinema*, Palgrave Studies in Arab Cinema, https://doi.org/10.1007/978-3-031-18858-9_7

This was the last time I entered Studio Al-Sakhra as the Israeli bombardment of the neighboring area of the Sports City made travel there impossible.

Upon Israeli's invasion of Lebanon in June of 1982, only the newly filmed material had not made it to the archived storage, as some recent footage was kept at the headquarters of the PCI or at Studio Al-Sakhra, where material for my film was left on the table during the editing process.

We sent some young men to Studio Al-Sakhra and asked them to bring back the footage that lay on the editing table. They reported that they only found a box next to the machine that contained a number of film reels from which we chose suitable shots for the film. The box was secured at a friend's studio until further work was possible. The material was lost a second time, but I do not feel it is appropriate to recount the story at length. This is how I lost two years of writing and shooting for a film on women and the revolution. What remains of the project is the notebook where I transcribed the audiotapes.

After Omar and Mutee' were martyred, Samir Nimr and Abu Thareef left for a filmmaking workshop in Moscow, along with Muwafaq who also received a scholarship in the Democratic German Republic. Many filmmakers and sound engineers, like Omar Al-Rashidi and Shaher Al-Soumi, were unable to reach the office of the PCI which was located in an area that was heavily and constantly bombed. Khalil Sa'adeh began working at the PLO Chairman's Office and returned every night to sleep at the PCI office.

At this point, our friends, the director Jean Chamoun and the newly arrived Mai Al Masri[1] (who recently graduated from university in the United States, looking forward to work with the PCI), expressed their willingness and desire to cover the events.

Mustafa and I lived with our two children at Jean's house in the first days of the invasion, then we moved to Bedford Hotel, which had been abandoned in Al-Hamra area. Mustafa handed Jean and Mai the camera and sound recorder he took from the office to cover the events. The material formed a large part of Jean Chamoun and Mai Masri's film *Under the Rubble* (1983).

---

[1] The recently graduated Palestinian director Mai Al Masri had come to the PCI shortly before the siege of Beirut in 1982. She married Jean Chamoun and they directed several films together. Then, she went on to direct her own films including *Children of Fire, Children of Shatila, Frontiers of Dreams and Fears*, and, most recently, her first feature fiction film, *3000 Nights*.

During that time, I was consumed by my work with the Union of Palestinian Women. I focused on securing emergency goods for the militants and those displaced from Southern Lebanon, and families living in West Beirut. Working with international organizations, I served at the time as the coordinator of the women and children's programs in the Palestinian camps. I tried as best as I could to balance my responsibilities toward my own children in the impossible times of the war.

ABU THAREEF RECALLS

"In 1980, Samir and I were sent to a training course on directing, but we returned in 1982 and documented the unfolding events. We would develop the footage in Damascus and secure a copy for safekeeping in the archive. At the end of the war, we went to Damascus and worked at the operations office for some time before heading back to Moscow. When we returned to Tunis in 1985, we were not able to continue our work as an institute, but we persisted in filming Palestinian events and activities. All our footage is kept at the archive of the cinema institute in Tunis."[2]

ATTEMPTS TO RESCUE MATERIAL, EQUIPMENT, AND ARCHIVE OF THE PALESTINIAN CINEMA INSTITUTION

During the limited hours of ceasefire, Mustafa and I moved the material that had been at the offices of the PCI during the siege of Beirut. We would cross to the office, which was in a heavily targeted area, and carry what we could of the remaining materials and equipment from there. We were surprised a number of times by the illuminating bombs that preceded air raids.

The bombardment during the siege of Beirut often lasted all day and night.[3] It did not stop until there was a ceasefire, which allowed the mediators to move between the Israeli forces, represented by the American negotiator Philip Habib, with the PLO leadership and Lebanese Nationalist Forces. These short breaks from the airstrikes lasted several hours, mostly during the night.

Mustafa and I would seize these moments of ceasefire after putting our children to sleep. Sometimes, only our younger son would be asleep, and the older one, who was eleven years old, would stay up to look after him.

---

[2] From Abu Thareef's interview, conducted by the author on August 15, 2016.
[3] The Israeli siege of Beirut lasted from June 4 until the end of August 1982, when the PLO forces started leaving Beirut on ships.

We would head toward the areas of Al Fakahani and the Arab University, where the cluster of buildings housing the offices of the PLO branches were located. We moved the remaining films, footage, and equipment to the archive storage which was safer.

Once, we tried to take advantage of the brief break from the insane airstrikes to head home, then to the PCI office, to gather what we could carry.

I recall that Mustafa carried another group of boxes (containing copies of films or film reels brought from the studio directly before the beginning of the events on June 4). He headed toward the stairs, and I grabbed more boxes and followed him. After descending a few steps, I felt a light emanating. These were the illuminating bombs dropped by the Israeli military planes to illuminate the targeted area before the actual bombing began. Mustafa and I were standing at their precise targeted spot. I was overtaken by a moment of panic, and screamed:

"Mustafaaaaaa. Quickly walk away from the building." My mind was racing at an unconceivable speed as I thought of our children, asleep in the hotel room. At least one of us must stay alive for their sake.

At the same time, I heard Mustafa scream, "Khadijah, get down quickly."

I rushed down the stairs, anxious that the bomb or rocket would land before I escaped. I repeated, "Leave quickly. Move away from the building."

We screamed at each other for a brief moment that felt very long because of the intense anxiety. This building and the ones around us were being targeted. This less than one-square-kilometer area housed the Unified Information, Palestine News Agency—Wafa, Fatah Revolutionary Council, Broadcast, and Foreign Relations Office.

As I reached the entrance of the building, I felt disbelief at having finally made it to the ground. I quickly lay down on the floor as we were taught in the training camps. The moment I composed myself and realized that I had safely left the building, I got up once more and ran toward our parked car. Mustafa was anxiously waiting for me there. When we safely arrived at our room in Al-Hamra, I discovered that my leg had been injured when I carelessly threw myself on the floor.

As for the film reels that were at Studio Al-Sakhra, the team that was sent to retrieve the material only found the footage disposed of during the editing process. It is likely that the material we were working on at the time was seized by the Israeli military that crossed the path toward Studio

Al-Sakhra during the first days of bombardment. No one had been able to reach the studio before the Israeli soldiers. Unfortunately, my second film *Women of My Country* also went missing. This film that I had been editing discusses the role and ambition of women during the revolution. It was co-produced by the PCI and the Union of Arab Documentarists. I had received confirmation of approved funding for this second film after my first one, *Children Without Childhood*, won a special mention from the jury at the Baghdad International Festival for Films and TV Programs on Palestine in 1980. I was the first Palestinian female director to make a film.

During the departure plans of the PLO forces to leave Beirut, we told three of the main PLO leaders about the location of the archive and provided them the names of the archive assistants and a cinematographer who would remain in Lebanon (they were able to stay because they carried IDs as Palestinian refugees in Lebanon). We were concerned that the archive could not be transported on the ships carrying the cadres and leadership of the PLO, because it was too vast. It occupied a space that was approximately 4 by 6 meters full of shelves lining the walls and in the middle of the room, containing cans of film negatives and positives, magnetic sound reels, in addition to our film library containing Palestinian films, revolutionary films from the Third World, and Palestine-solidarity groups. We learned later that the cinema archive was placed under the protection of the French Embassy when the leadership was not able to secure it aboard the ship. We pursued news of the archive and the possibility of transporting it outside of Beirut for three years. We were informed of some failed attempts to move it to Cyprus.

We continued to be in touch by phone with our colleague and the archive assistants who remained in Beirut, to follow up on the situation there and on the conditions of the archive. This lasted until mid-1985, when the War of the Camps signaled worsening conditions of the Lebanese civil war, and all embassies closed their doors.

Then at some point, the French Embassy alerted our contact about the necessity of moving the archive because the embassy was shutting down.

Our contact told us that there was no appropriate space, and several ideas were suggested including the Gaza Hospital, the Palestinian Red Crescent, or any other hospital or mosque. Finally, a Lebanese merchant close to Fatah offered a storage space in the area of Bir Hassan, and some of the militants volunteered to transport the archive.

Our contact later told us that he was detained by the Amal movement, and the Lebanese merchant was imprisoned by the Syrians during the War of the Camps perpetrated by the Amal movement, with backing from Syria. After he and the Lebanese merchant were released, they didn't find the archive in its place.

There were some rumors here and there, but none of them amounted to anything about the archive that had documented this important period of Palestinian struggle. The archive contains both the films of the Palestine Film Unit/Palestinian Cinema Institution and the films of the cinematheque. Because of its disappearance, it is largely unknown among today's younger generations.

If I were to speculate about the mystery of its disappearance, I would say that it still exists somewhere under the custody of a state, organization, or institution that has a primary interest in hiding this rich and important cinematic heritage of the Palestinian people.

It is impossible for an archive of this size to disappear completely without leaving behind any trace. Even if the storage place was bombed, exploded, or subjected to vandalism or open fire, pieces of the archive were preserved to resist melting and withering away completely.

DISPERSION ONCE MORE

The PCI team dispersed to different parts of the Arab world after the PLO forces left Lebanon. No country would bear the responsibility of hosting the entire organization. The officials of the political, information, and cultural offices spread to Syria, Jordan, Algeria, Cyprus, Sudan, and Yemen, while Tunis welcomed the leadership of the PLO and a limited number of the cadres. Those working at the PCI also dispersed. Some received academic scholarships like our colleague Muwafaq (Marwan Salameh) who went to the Democratic German Republic to study filmmaking. Samir and Abu Thareef were together outside for a training course as Abu Thareef previously mentioned, while others went back to Jordan, Syria, or Egypt where they had previously lived.

Some PCI filmmakers joined the PLO leadership and cadres at the headquarters in Tunis, where they worked under the Unified Information Office. They continued filming Palestinian activities, events, and the leadership of the PLO in Tunis. The colleagues of the PCI managed to produce two films: the first in 1983 entitled *The Longest of The Days*, and the second in 1988 entitled *The Last Fifteen Minutes* directed by Mohammad Al-Sawalmeh. The director Mohammad Tawfiq also made *The Child and the Toy* in 1986. It was impossible for the work to continue as it had before when the PCI had an independent specialized administration, and the absence of so many filmmakers was deeply felt.

The department of Culture and Information of the PLO continued to work from its headquarters in Damascus for a few more years. It supported some film projects for directors working under the framework of the PLO. For example, Qais Al-Zubeidi made *Palestine: A People's Record* in 1982, *The Confrontation* in 1983, and *Massacre* in 1984. Hikmat Daoud directed *Forever in Our Memory* in 1982. Yahya Barakat directed *Abu Salma* in 1982. Qasem Hawal made *The Identity* in 1984. Mohammad Tawfiq made *Um Ali* (Ali's Mother) and *Al-Natour* (The Guard) in 1988. And there were other film projects up to the end of 1990.

We left Beirut after an exhausting siege and war that bombarded West Beirut, where the offices of the PLO were located. For more than eighty infamous days, the PLO's political and military powers resisted, attempting to protect the city from attack and surrendered in the face of the destructive IDF bombing from ground, sea, and sky.

Those of us who survived did so by chance or through experience gained from previous battles in maneuvering amid gunfire, barrels bombs, and airstrikes. That experience taught us, for example, that if a strike came from a barge in the sea, it could penetrate a wall, but one could hide in the internal hallways of apartment buildings. If the strike came from heavy artillery on top of a mountain, it is preferable to hide in a shelter or at least the apartment's staircase. If the strike came from airplanes, it's best to exit the building for the street, and this is what I used to do with my children, go out to the street.

We left wounded and scarred on the soul level. It was difficult to believe that we had made it out alive. I personally felt for the first time as if I were living "like a feather in the wind," when we were forced to leave everything we had accomplished behind.

When we gathered our fragmented souls, each in a different place, we realized it would be impossible to rebuild the Palestinian Cinema Institution in exile. It was also impossible to rescue the archive that remained under the custody of an ally state.

There no longer remained a stable and suitable place for the forces of the struggle, away from their homeland and popular base.

Mustafa decided at the time to work independently, hoping to achieve his goal of making a fiction film, specifically working on the script of *The Pessoptimist* (A*l Mutashail*). But there was no way for a director who chose the most difficult path to achieve his dreams after living in forced residence without a passport for fifteen years.

BIBLIOGRAPHY

Interview with Abu Thareef conducted on August 15th, 2016

CHAPTER 8

Search for the Lost Films of the Palestinian Cinema Institution

The idea of the search began in 2004 when Mustafa settled in Ramallah and worked to re-establish the Palestinian Cinema Group. He proposed the project of re-establishing the cinematheque (film library) and searching for the lost Palestinian films in the cinema archive in 2006.

The search for the archive of the Palestinian Cinema Institution could not occur openly and publicly, because it was not lost by coincidence or as a result of negligence. The archive was, to put it simply, stolen as a result of the complications of the Lebanese Civil War and the War of the Palestinian Camps (1985–1987) that restrained the mobility of Palestinians. The Palestinians were not able to protect the archive, and frankly, present circumstances do not permit narrating the full story.

The search was limited to looking for the films of the Palestinian revolution, especially the PCI films lost with the archive, because we had learned that other Palestinian organizations that produced films were able to move them in suitcases from Beirut to Damascus, and the originals and copies of the films of the Department of Culture and Information of the PLO were available in Damascus.

The project was presented to a number of European and Arab donors, but it only succeeded in obtaining a conditional promise of funds from the audiovisual department at the French Consulate in Jerusalem. They agreed to allocate funds to be donated after receiving information about the expected number of films and their locations. We did not have that information at the time, and we needed to conduct a preliminary search.

© The Author(s), under exclusive license to Springer Nature Switzerland AG 2023
K. Habashneh, *Knights of Cinema*, Palgrave Studies in Arab Cinema, https://doi.org/10.1007/978-3-031-18858-9_8

In the beginning of the search, Mustafa Abu Ali died from an unexpected illness, and the new administrative body of the Palestinian Cinema Group could not follow up on the project after he passed away.

I personally resumed the search for possible locations or institutions that housed copies of the films. My previous experience as the head of the archive and cinematheque at the PCI between 1976 and 1982 was very valuable in this respect. I also benefited from my trusted connections with Palestinian officials of the PLO, especially officials from the global offices of the PLO who understand and appreciate the value of the films I was searching for.

I started the search in motion at the beginning of 2010 in collaboration with the Palestine National Fund. We did not receive any response about copies of the films until the beginning of 2011, when I was invited to the Palestinian Embassy in Morocco to search through a huge number of film reels they stored. I searched among more than sixty reels of film, in coordination with the Moroccan Cinema Center. I found very few films produced by other global directors. The Palestinian films were mostly full of cuts, and there were three or more copies of *Tal Al-Za'atar* which used to be lent out and screened at schools, universities, and cineclubs.

The search was conducted between phone calls, emails, and trips to several countries where the PCI produced or exchanged films. All the Palestinian embassies (former offices of the PLO) were contacted several times and at different intervals. Committees for solidarity with Palestine and allied cinema groups were also contacted, as were the directors and filmmakers who had made films about the Palestinian cause. In sum, around 100 contacts were conducted with embassies, committees, collectives, companies, studios, and workshops, until by mid-2016, I had collected 40 films or film reels made by the PFU/PCI, several copies of films co-produced with progressive filmmakers who were friends of the PCI, and films made by other Palestinian organizations. In the end, I collected more than 60 films.

After I started searching for the lost films, I learned that the Italian Audiovisual Archive of the Democratic Workers Movement (AAMOD) had inherited the archive of the Italian Communist Party, and the German filmmaker Monica Maurer is working with AAMOD. I felt relieved about that, as Monica was a friend to the PCI: she came to Beirut in 1978, and 1979 many times, and worked on a number of films with the PCI crew. In July 2012, I wrote her to tell her that, we, the PLO, had started searching for PCI films, and that I was thinking of coming to Rome to search for the films Mustafa had left there and to look for studios or labs for film digitiza-tion. As soon as I could, in September 2013, I went there to meet with the administration of AAMOD to search mainly for the original copy of *Tal Al-Za'atar* and the PCI film footage that Mustafa had left in the custody of Unitelefilm with the Italian Communist Party. He had done this hoping to later transport it back to the PCI in Beirut, as he mentioned in his letter on the work on *Tal Al-Za'atar*, dated October 8, 1977.[1]

It is likely that the footage can be found among what AAMOD inher-ited from the archive of the Communist Party. Once I was in Rome, accompanied by the cultural attaché of the Palestinian embassy, Mustafa Al Qadoumi, I met with Monica, who was on the administrative board of AAMOD and was appointed to meet me. I learned from her that they had recently found the Italian copy of *Tal Al-Za'atar* and some of the footage that remained from work on *Tal Al-Za'atar* film. The material was found in a deplorable condition, especially the magnetic sound tapes that included a recording of the interview I had conducted with the militant Abdelmuhsin Al-Za'atar (Nabil Ma'rouf), the political leader of the battle of Tal Al-Za'atar. I had also learned that they were able to secure funding, with support from the Palestinian artist Emily Jacir, who was living in Rome and helped Monica on the film material. They planned to deposit a copy of the material at the Institute for Palestine Studies in Beirut and Ramallah. Monica said that they are not allowed to give any copy to any-one else, because the rights of the footage belong now to the donors of the footage restoration.

The purpose of my visit to Rome, to meet the AAMOD people, was mainly to search for the original negative of *Tal Al-Za'atar*, which to my knowledge should be in the Cinecitta (Cinema City) laboratory. Unfortunately, the AAMOD representative couldn't help with this. Monica said that we cannot ask Cinecittà about the original of the film, even if they still have it, because they will ask for storage fees of more than thirty years. To my knowledge and from our experience, the film studios and laboratories traditionally keep the originals of the films they print, as it is their right to print copies for the producers of the films. This was my experience in Lebanon with Studio Ba'albak and in London with Filmatic Studio where I made visual effects for my film *Children Without Childhood*, the original of which I kept there. Perhaps Italian studios have different traditions.

---

[1] This letter can be found in Appendix B.

At the beginning of 2015, I was surprised to learn of a screening of *Tal Al-Zaʿatar* in Arabic organized by the cultural organization, Darat Al Funun, in Amman, which revealed that it had supported the costs of restoring the material that had been found in the AAMOD archive. I then learned from Monica that they had only found the original Arabic (Palestinian) audio of the film?! They were able to sync the Arabic soundtrack with the Italian copy of the film. How could they find only the original Arabic soundtrack of *Tal Al-Zaʿatar* without the picture reel? This seemed strange to me.

Usually after the process of mixing the soundtracks of a film, the original reels are interlocked together while all the tracks of the film (picture, sounds, and visual effects) are synchronized before printing onto one master print.

Overall and unfortunately, the AAMOD archive did not know about the nature of the film materials they inherited from the Italian Communist Party that dissolved at the beginning of the 1990s, until the end of 2012 or beginning of 2013. This is after we had started working on collecting the films and searching around for the original negatives and copies of PCI films.

The film materials of *Tal Al-Zaʿatar* were left in 1977. The rushes and outtakes that were left with Unitelefilm and Cinecittà (Cinema City) after the work on the film was done were found in very poor condition because they had not been classified and preserved properly. They had been neglected for more than thirty years, from 1977 until they were discovered.

In the summer of 2015, while I was searching for the films of the PCI, I received a phone call from the militant Daoud Barakat who had worked as the head of the PLO Office in Geneva during the 1970s and 1980s. He insisted on getting in touch after learning about my efforts to search for and collect the lost films of the PCI, suggesting that he had information that would be useful for the search. When we met, he informed me that during one of his visits to Beirut at the end of 1981 or the beginning of 1982, he had received a call from Mustafa who inquired about the possibility of leaving several films of the PCI for safekeeping in the Swiss Cinema Archive that had recently been established in Switzerland. And as it so happens, Daoud added that he had returned to Geneva with fifteen films from the PCI, which he deposited at the cinematheque in Switzerland.

Daoud and I started reviewing the names, phone numbers, and addresses of friends and comrades who were living in Switzerland at the time, looking for ways to initiate a search for the films. I contacted the administration of the Swiss Cinematheque in Lausanne, which was under renovation, and we were delayed for some time because of this. The process of the search lasted nearly two years, as we were able, through communication with the administration of the cinematheque in Lausanne, to recover only four of the original fifteen films. I think the cinematheque was unable to locate the films because of the difficulty in identifying an accurate date when the films were deposited, and the titles under which they were labeled, in addition to being poorly organized since its beginnings in the early 1980s. I didn't ask for copies of the films the cinematheque claimed to have found, because I already had copies of them. This issue requires further follow-up.

The journey in search of the films was a difficult one, and it consumed about a decade of effort. During that time, I was the planning and execution manager, and the secretary who typed and responded to letters. I carried the film reels that arrived through the Palestinian embassies and looked for a 16 mm projector or 16 mm editing machine (Moviola) to watch the films, check their contents, and assess the degree of damage that had accumulated over time and in the absence of proper preservation conditions. Currently it is very difficult to find 16 mm machines because everything is digital, especially in Jordan where there is no cinema industry. Although filmmaking began there before the start of the television industry, it was stopped in the beginning of the 1970s. It took a long time before I discovered that the Jordanian Television had repaired an old editing machine, as a means to search for some old films. I collaborated with them by coordinating the search with the Palestinian embassy in Jordan. Unfortunately, we were obliged to move the films to Cairo to continue watching and cleaning the films.

At the end of 2018, in an old office of Fatah in Cairo, I accidently found two film reels, and what I suspect is *Newsreel No. 3* and a copy of the film *The Key*, which I hope is in Arabic. I have many copies of the film prepared in different languages, such as French, German, and Spanish. I have not yet seen the reels because they were discovered the day before I left. They are kept under paid custody, alongside a Palestinian (Arabic) copy of the film *Tal Al-Za'atar* at the Cinema Company (formerly the Sound, Light and Cinema company) that is now affiliated with the National Cinema Institute in the area of Al-Haram [in Giza].

Most of the films that were produced nearly forty years ago were found buried in storage or forgotten cellars amid dust and rust. At the end, we were able to find 80 percent of the films whose negatives were lost with the archive. And the journey in search for funding to restore the films ensued. A number of successive ministers of culture were contacted, and every national Palestinian organization and institute related to culture was contacted to contribute funding. All of them, however, have budgets limited for their own programs.

A few films have been digitized, restored, and translated through personal initiatives because they were in demand at forums and festivals of Palestinian films around the world. The film *They Do Not Exist* and *Newsreel No.1* were digitized and color-corrected through support from the Palestine National Fund in 2014. *With Soul, With Blood* and *Scenes from the Occupation of Gaza* were digitized and restored in collaboration with the French Cinematheque.

Some films were never missing. *Palestine in the Eye* was found with Hani Jawharieh's family. *Palestinian Visions* and *Children Without Childhood* were with their directors, Adnan Madanat, and myself, respectively. After participating in the Moscow Film Festival in July 1981, Madanat and I arrived in Beirut right after the Israeli air raids on Al Fakahani, when the PCI was thinking of moving the archive to a safer place. This is the only reason why our films were spared.

In mid-2013, I started to hear whispers of news from the Israeli art historian Rona Sela, who suggested that there is a strong possibility the lost Palestinian Cinema Institution archive is housed in the Israeli Army Archive, which was inaccessible to researchers and historians unlike other archives in Israel. I had also heard this from the Israeli director Eyal Sivan when I participated in the London Palestine Film Festival in 2007. Sela made a film in 2017 entitled *Looted and Hidden,* and an extensive article about the topic by Israeli writer Ofer Aderet was published in *Haaretz* newspaper under the title "Why Are Countless Palestinian Photos and Films Buried in Israeli Archives?" on July 1, 2017. Then, Sela published a book about the Israeli Army's theft of everything related to Palestinian cultural and political heritage, entitled *Made Public,*[2] especially after she found and conducted an interview with one of the soldiers who helped transport the archives of the PLO Office in Beirut in 1982.

The investigation and search for the missing archive is ongoing until further notice (Figs. 8.1 and 8.2).

---

[2] Rona Sela, *li-Mo'ayyinat il-jumhour: hikayat suwwar filastiniyah 'mo'taqilah' fil archiffat al-askariyyeh israiliyyah [For the Public]* (Ramallah: Madar Institute, 2018): its title in Arabic differs from the English translation, *Made in Public,* from the Hebrew original.

Fig. 8.1 Khadijeh watching old film reels at the Moroccan Cinema Center while searching, July 2011

Fig. 8.2 Khadijeh watching films at the French Cinematheque, June 4, 2016

CORRECTING MISCONCEPTIONS ABOUT THE PALESTINIAN CINEMA ARCHIVE

Recently, toward the second decade of the twenty-first century, some people have confused films of the Palestinian Revolution for archival films. This betrays a misunderstanding about the difference between the footage that documents an event or topic and films that have a specific message of the director through form and vision.

There is an idea spread around that the archive of Palestinian cinema is dispersed in many places. In reality, this narrative is misleading because it reveals a misunderstanding of what an archive actually is and overlooks the fact that the original archive is lost and the process of looking for it is impeded. It gives the impression that all we must do is re-assemble these dispersed pieces of film to save the archive of Palestinian cinema.

The archive of Palestinian cinema, which is the archive of revolutionary cinema, is lost. It is an archive that was categorized, organized, and covered all the political and military events of the Palestinian revolution and all popular mobilizations like strikes, protests, festivals, conferences, and campaigns to secure the needs of the people during military combat and war. It also covered cultural and social activities and all that surrounded the activities and organizations of the PLO, spanning fifteen years, from the public launch of the Palestinian revolution in 1968 until 1982. This is what is called the archive of Palestinian cinema, or archive of Palestinian revolutionary cinema.

In this context of the archive, there is only one general archive for Palestinian cinema, which is the archive of the Palestinian Cinema Institution. This archive is lost, and there is an urgency to retrieve it.

The lost archive includes around 90 films from the cinematheque (film library). It is comprised of the missing films of the Palestinian Cinema Institution (we worked to retrieve copies of many of them) and other films from other liberation moments and revolutionary countries and organizations. However, the archive of Palestinian cinema is not merely films or unused film footage.

It is true that there might be an audiovisual archive of the Department of Culture and Information of the PLO that houses originals and copies of the films it produced in Beirut and Damascus. There are also, no doubt, private archives for Palestinian organizations that document their activities like private conferences, interviews, and speeches by the leadership, and activities of the organization.

However, all these particular archives do not constitute what we can call the archive of Palestinian cinema. These archives are specific to Palestinian organizations, and they could be considered complementary to the archive of the PCI. These archives were not lost, since their small size allowed them to be transported in a number of suitcases, as I heard from a member of the PFLP leadership, Salah Salah, when I met him in mid-June of 2016 in Beirut. I informed the leadership and the main film-maker of the PFLP, Qasem Hawal, when I received copies of some of their films and asked what to do with them. Hawal suggested preparing a joint archiving project, and the topic was discussed several times but there was no real initiative from him or the PFLP to work collectively on archiving the films of the revolutionary period. While writing this book, I heard from a member of the Political Office of the PFLP that they already saved their films.

A large number of filmmakers visited the Palestinian revolution and produced films about the Palestinian cause from different perspectives. Certainly, not all of the footage they documented was used (we call these outtakes). In addition, material from the archive of the PCI was often provided to supplement loose footage that was captured to portray a specific topic. These are important materials to be collected and cared for and might be of use to the archive of Palestinian cinema.

But neither outtakes nor fragmentary footage used selectively in films can be considered part of the archive of Palestinian cinema if they are not organized and classified. The missing archive is not just film material, but a methodically structured system of organizing the material, working in close proximity to the mission of the PCI. Its loss constitutes the loss of an irreplaceable institutional record.

The widespread idea about the dispersion of the archive of Palestinian cinema in reality points to fragmented footage that was captured at different moments, mostly in the second half of the 1970s, by tens of filmmakers who recorded footage or directed films about the Palestinian cause. Some filmmakers still have some fragments of this footage, and if they are not categorized and preserved in a suitable place, they can become damaged.

I contacted directors who produced films in collaboration with the PCI about copies of their films and the remaining footage. I learned from many that what remained of the footage was not cared for because it was not considered valuable, as the important shots were incorporated into the films. Some said that the additional footage was damaged or lost as time passed and things were moved from one place to another. I learned this from the French director Guy Chapouillie, who edited *The Olive Tree* and *Ezzedine Qalaq* when I asked about the interview with the martyr Ezzedine Qalaq that was selectively used in the film about his life and works. I had conducted this interview with him (Qalaq) myself in 1977, as part of the archive's initiative to document the experience of the revolution's leaders and distinguished cadres.

Where to Find Important Material and Footage of the PCI Archive

It is very important to get a copy of these scattered film documents to preserve at the archive of the Palestinian National Library, as part of the Palestinian Cinema Archive. The rights over these documents belong to the Palestinian people, the PLO, and its representatives.

Firstly

A copy of the cinema archive specific to the PLO political organizations, and the department of Culture and Information, must be preserved at the Palestinian National Library because it is part of the history of the Palestinian people.

Secondly

The Audiovisual Archive of the Democratic Workers Movement (AAMOD), which inherited the cinema archive of the Italian Communist Party, has a large amount of remaining film material belonging to the PCI that was left in Rome with Unitelefilm in 1977. This material is important because it includes the negative of the Arabic copy of *Tal Al-Za'atar* and remaining outtakes that did not make it into the film, in addition to about

10,000 meters of film reels covering the events of the Lebanese Civil War which were marked for use for a film about Beirut. All of this material was left in Rome, as the film's director Mustafa Abu Ali notes in his article "Snapshots of the Cinematic Experience During the Lebanese War (1975-1976)"[3] and his letters following up on the work. No doubt the director Monica Maurer has some of the outtakes and remaining material from the films she made in collaboration with the PCI. All the material speculated to be found in the archive of AAMOD or with Monica Maurer documents the events of the war in Lebanon and the Israeli invasion of Southern Lebanon between 1976 and 1982.

Thirdly
A number of PCI films co-produced with the Tunisian Cinema Institute (SATBAC) in the 1970s are held at the Tunisian cinema archive alongside footage covering events and activities of the PLO during its stay in Tunis from 1982 to 1994. After communicating with the administration of the archive, we received a list of available Palestinian films and footage, and we agreed on retrieving the material when it is convenient for both parties.

Fourthly
The search for the group of films that was deposited at the Swiss Cinematheque in Switzerland through the Palestine Office in Geneva in 1981 or 1982 must resume. There is a total of fifteen negative reels (as noted in a letter from the head of the PCI to Studio Ba'albak reproduced in Appendix G at the end of this book).[4]

Concluding Remarks

I hope I have successfully narrated the story of the Palestine Film Unit/ Palestinian Cinema Institution, clarifying the circumstances of its films and archive.

I have dedicated all my efforts to researching the information that was not available, and to remaining true to the story of the unit while avoiding any personal feelings toward those who worked at or with the PCI.

---

[3] Mustafa Abu Ali, *Palestinian Image* magazine, First issue (Beirut: Palestinian Cinema Institution, 1978).

[4] This letter is Fig. G.21 in Appendix G—Photographs Documenting the Palestine Film Unit and Palestinian Cinema Institution.

I feel that I must point out that the experience of the unit aligned with the experience of the Palestinian revolution and perhaps the experiences of other revolutions. Its beginnings differ from its final moments, or perhaps what we may call its end.

The pioneers began by carrying the message and the cause of their people, and their just struggle to liberate their homeland from Israeli settler colonialism. They derived inspiration from the militant fedayee's infinite sacrifice and selflessness as they innovated a new cinematic language that corresponded with the reality of their revolution and its people.

The experience of the pioneers and those who joined them was distinguished by a spirit of groupwork, humility, modesty, and equality in the right to participate in order to safeguard the path of struggle and revolution. Though the PFU/PCI lost, through its struggle, two of the founders of the Palestine Film Unit, those who were not martyred, stayed true to the message and surged with it toward global horizons. Palestinian revolutionary cinema became one of the hallmarks of militant cinema around the world.

When a movement for national liberation makes progress, starts achieving its goals, and attracts attention to its singularity, as happened with the Palestinian revolutionary cinema, its concepts and standards evolve in their value and applicability. The example of this is the evolution of the Palestinian Cinema Institution from the origins, energy, and struggles of the Palestine Film Unit and those who participated in the Palestinian revolution. But the modesty and equality in opportunity which formed the basis of sacrifice at the beginning of the PCI and which motivated plans for filmmaking and training workshops to improve the standards of film production were difficult to maintain over time in the development of the work. This was reflected in the productions of the PCI and other revolutionary organizations in later years, for which a scientific and professional work plan became necessary to advance the journey of work and struggle, in combination with developing the concept and technical elements of the films.

We began with certain values and grew to international prominence, but we needed to raise the qualitative standards of our work with more attention to scientific and strategic planning. History interfered and stopped this effort, and now we are in the process of retrieving and preserving what remains from the whole experience.

BIBLIOGRAPHY

Sela, Rona. *li-Mo'ayyinat il-Jumhour: Hikayat Suwwar Filastiniyah 'Mo'taqilah' fil Archiffat al-Askariyyah Israiliyah [For the Public]*. Ramallah: Al-Madar, Al-Markez Al- Filastin lil Dirasat Al- Israiliyah, 2018.

Al-Surah al-Filastiniyah [Palestinian Image], First issue, Beirut: Muassaset al-Sinima al-Filastiniyah, 1978.

APPENDIX A: MANIFESTOS FROM THE PALESTINE FILM UNIT AND PALESTINIAN CINEMA GROUP

PALESTINE FILM UNIT MANIFESTO

Issued on the occasion of the First International Festival for Youth Cinema/Damascus, April 1972.

"Militant Cinema"

Militant cinema is what expresses the people's struggle and conveys its militant experiences to the world. This benefits the people themselves, and all militant movements worldwide.

The Palestinian struggle materializes a new reality with new characteristics that emphasize themselves in all aspects of Palestinian life. Through this reality, a new Palestinian art is crystallizing across artistic specializations including poetry, storytelling, fine arts, music and theatre. It also materializes in cinema.

Palestinian cinema, which is necessarily a militant cinema, is still in the early stages of its development. Yet the least one can say is that it has taken steps in the right direction towards transforming film into a weapon added to the arsenal of the Palestinian revolution and revolutionary movements worldwide.

The nascent Palestinian cinema is aware, at least as represented by those working under the name "Palestine Films" that it must express the spirit of the armed struggle of the people, criticize the corrupt and backwards reality and plant the values of the people's war of liberation. This culminates in the right of self-determination for the Palestinian people on their land.

© The Author(s), under exclusive license to Springer Nature Switzerland AG 2023
K. Habashneh, *Knights of Cinema*, Palgrave Studies in Arab Cinema, https://doi.org/10.1007/978-3-031-18858-9

Militant Palestinian cinema must find new tools and frameworks capable of capturing the glorious struggle of the Palestinian people. The peoples' cinema must express the peoples' war.

Militant cinema has specific values and standards that differ from traditional cinema. As such, the values and standards must not be confused. The value of a militant film is measured by its benefit to the revolutionary cause of the film.

Palestinian militant cinema does not pose a geographic affiliation but an affiliation with the Palestinian revolutionary cause.

Long live the struggle of the people towards liberation.
Long live the armed struggle.
Long live the militant revolution.
—Palestine Films

PALESTINIAN CINEMA GROUP MANIFESTO

Issued during the First Baghdad International Festival for Films and TV Programs on Palestine, March 1973.

Arab cinema has, for some time, been consumed by topics that do not engage with reality or perhaps offer superficial treatment of it. With time, the Arab viewer has become accustomed to forms that have contributed, in one shape or another, to numbing his consciousness and driving him further away from important issues in confronting Zionist imperialism and Arab backwardness.

Throughout the journey of Arab cinema, several ambitious attempts at expressing reality stand out. However, these attempts have quickly disappeared under the pressure of cinema monopolies working with full awareness and intentionality to prevent the emergence of a meaningful Arab cinema. The development of political events has pushed for the necessity of a new cinema. However, it has engaged on the level of events but not on the level of ambition. As such, it has been revisionist in its subject matter, but remains deeply entrenched in the forms of traditional cinema. The depth of the June 1967 defeat has defined the abilities of the devout youth who believe in people and has launched them towards producing films carrying the characteristics of alternative cinema in both subject matter and form. These films have addressed the defeat and reflect the steadfast position of the people, confidently portraying the Palestinian cause and the armed resistance of the Arab Palestinian people.

This reflects the importance of Palestinian cinema and the need for its development so that it can stand alongside the courageous fighters, to film the stages of the Arab peoples' struggle to liberate their land, and to reflect the past and present while envisioning the future. Such a cinema must grow and develop through organized efforts because individual efforts will remain limited.

Those of us who are interested in issues of cinema, literature, and thought, have written this statement to express the importance of organizing a cinema group we have called the "Palestinian Cinema Group" based on the following ideals and principles:

1. The group aims to produce Palestinian films committed to the cause of the Palestinian revolution and its goals with a democratic Arab outlook.
2. The group works towards an alternative cinematic form that engages dialectically with the content.
3. The group directs its efforts and productions in service of the Palestinian revolution and the cause of the Palestinian Arab people.
4. The group considers itself among the institutions of the Palestinian revolution, so its funding comes from agreements with Palestinian or Arab parties that believe in its cause and aims. It invites the Palestine National Fund, or its representatives, to audit its financial activities.
5. The group will be based at the Palestine Research Center offices in Beirut.
6. The group will develop a workplan and internal policy to organize its internal and external relations.
7. The group's work objectives are:

   Production: To produce revolutionary films that rally the masses around the revolution and introduce the cause and the struggle of our people to the world.
   Documentation: To establish a cinema library (archive, to include still and moving images that express our peoples' struggle and the stages of the development of its cause).
   Collaboration: To strengthen and consolidate relationships with progressive and revolutionary cinema collectives worldwide. To represent Palestine at film festivals, and to offer film facilities to ally groups working to support the aims of the Palestinian revolution.

Long live the Palestinian revolution.
Baghdad, March 1973

Appendix B: Letters from Mustafa Sent During the Editing of *Tal Al-Za'atar*

September 17, 1977

My dear Khadijah,

What I have feared has happened, the delay.... Instead of finishing and releasing the first copy of the film, the work has been on hold since Pino returned from Budapest. Relations between us have been tense, and the agreement has nearly crumbled.

There was a meeting that included Nimr Hammad and Salati, the head of Middle East relations at the party... Then things started to improve, however the work remains on hold. We are ready for [sound] mixing, but we should probably wait until we solve the problem with Pino and Unitelefilm.

Time moves by with fatal slowness. Each minute feels like a slow and heavy day... Oh, how I wish you were with me now ... but the wind blows....

It is still unclear when we will be completely done. Things move slowly despite our insistence, Jean and I, on moving forward as quickly as possible. I don't want this production to fall through, so I have tolerated more than one should.

In any case, I comfort myself by thinking that we have waited a lot and will wait a bit more. I recently decided to finish at least the Arabic copy, but even this requires time. For example, the Letraset needs a week to arrive from Milan. Then I need three days, to write the titles.... Then I need God knows how many days in the lab... It would be great if we finish

© The Author(s), under exclusive license to Springer Nature Switzerland AG 2023
K. Habashneh, *Knights of Cinema*, Palgrave Studies in Arab Cinema, https://doi.org/10.1007/978-3-031-18858-9

by the first week of October... I fear that things will drag for another month... I am tired of the oppression and the delays...

I received a telegram from Mutee' who informed me of the impossibility of sending money to cover our living expenses, for Jean and I. This truly irritated me. In any case, this is our movement (Fatah) and we are used to this type of disregard. I will borrow some money for us and we'll get by, even if we're forced to beg if we don't find someone to lend to us.

***

September 19, 1977
Khadijah, my dear,

I received the letter you sent with Nimr's sister. It is the only thing that arrived. I beg you to write to me.... And please send to the Cosmopolitina address.

I explained to Mutee', in a letter I sent with Nimr's sister, all the recent developments and reasons for delay. Please refer to it so that I don't have to repeat the same topic.

We have now reached a roadblock. There is no way forward except if we make the decision to break off this agreement and cover the production costs entirely, which involves cutting ties and taking a financial decision (asking for money from the movement). I asked Mutee' to send me the decision by telegram as soon as possible. I urge you to put pressure for a quick decision because the situation has become hell for Jean and I.

***

Rome, September 23–24, 1977
Khadijah, my wife and dear,

I just got back from the Pantheon square with Jean, Rita, and Stefano. There was a music festival in the square organized by the socialist party. Before that, we stopped at the post office to send you a telegram asking for a response on whether we can cover 25 percent of the production costs. Our partners are pushing us to cancel the agreement or to accept conditions that are not in our favor, especially now that they have suggested making a special Italian copy, aiming to keep the archive here.

Since you left, they have been holding onto Pino's very silly stance. I mean his position, but also his persona itself. Despite the meetings that have included Salati and Nimr Hammad ... and all the rest of them (as I informed you in the previous letter). Nothing is produced yet and they always circle back to the same point, which is the need to please Pino in any way possible, even if it comes at the expense of the production. When I asked them, does it also "come at the expense of the film?" They responded: yes, Pino's opinion is our opinion. I suspect that this is all a tactic to push us to cancel the agreement, and it is confirmed by the letter they sent us asking to stop the work.

The film has been ready for mixing since almost the beginning of September, and we have learned that there are forces from within the party that are against us. The effect of Natoli's departure has been to delay our work as a first step, and to push for the cancellation of the agreement as a second step. Even when Natoli was in charge, he was always cautious not to express his support for us too vocally, perhaps fearing from some powers in the party that were unsympathetic to us.

What kills me is this delay. We wasted three weeks with no results, and I suspect the delay could drag for another three months. They are at home, the cause is not their cause, and they all have their own work to be concerned with. We heard from behind the scenes that in reality they are not interested in this production, and this has been repeated several times. In addition, we heard that Unitelefilm is collapsing, and we do not know the causes, but they are likely political.

The trust between us has been shaken, especially after Natoli left and Mazali replaced him. Jean calls him Mazali, or Mathaleh (meaning humiliation in Arabic). Jean and I feel that even if this agreement moves forward, the lack of trust will continue to delay the work in future on issues related to the distribution, archive, and everything.

I will stop here as I await the telegram. I am about to explode from the delay....

I hope that letter will help clarify the situation to the institute, and will contribute to making the decision to cover the 25 percent, or fully cover the production, if the decision has not already been made before this letter arrives.

Goodbye, with love
Mustafa

***

October 8, 1977
Khadijeh,
I write to you after all this delay which is beginning to give way to a solution. We are in the final stages of solving the problems, and it's fair to say that we've been 90 percent successful, and the problem has been completely solved with the agreement of both sides.

Based on this, Jean and I have agreed that I will travel after the mixing of the film, and he will stay and wait for the zero copy because one of us needs to be around and Jean speaks French, so his presence is more useful, especially that the next steps after the mixing are technical.

If there are no emergencies—on their part—I expect to be back in Beirut between October 16–20 at the latest. I will inform you by telegram of the exact date, and I will bring back the camera, and perhaps it is preferable to leave the films here, and to send someone from the institute to bring them back and return with Jean Chamoun. The exact arrangements can be made then, and all the films will be ready at once.

Back to work now. With great love, and kisses to you and 'Ammar. We will meet soon. Pass my regards to the institute,
Mustafa
(Figs. B.1, B.2, B.3, B.4, B.5, and B.6)

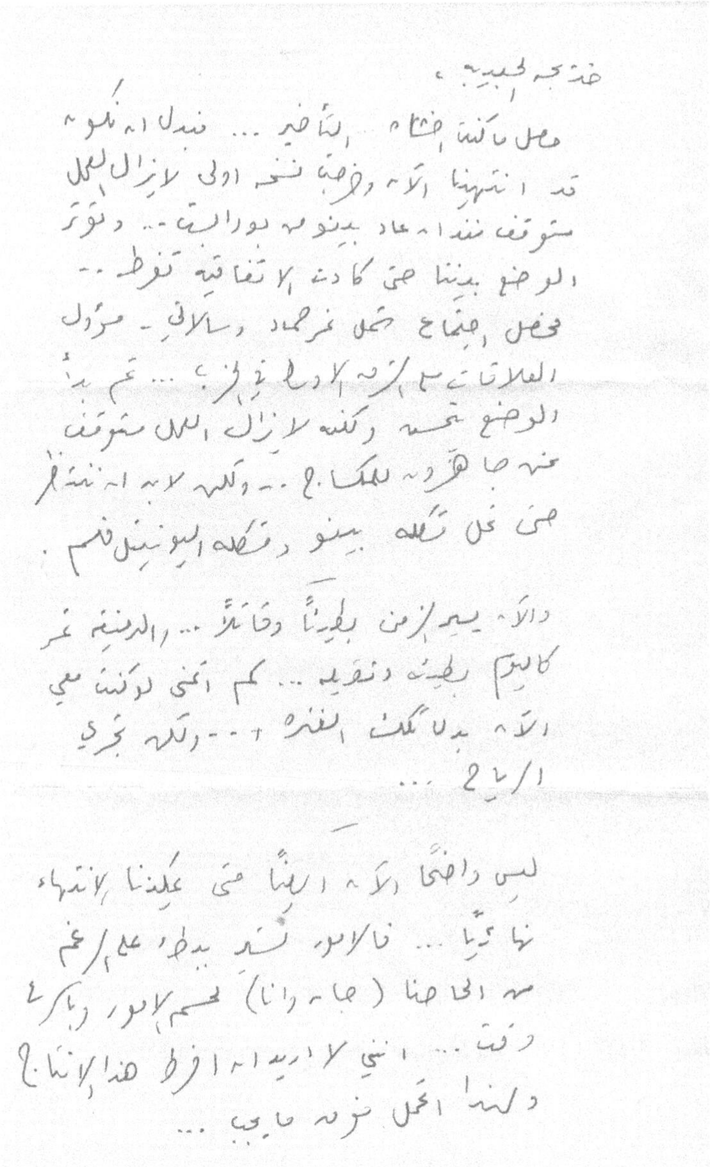

Fig. B.1   Arabic letter from Mustafa (above), September 17, 1977

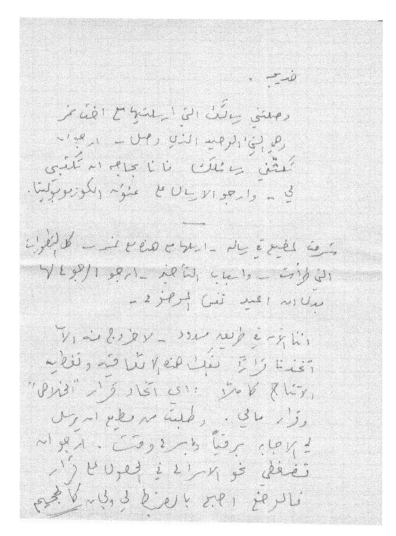

Fig. B.2 Arabic letter from Mustafa (above), September 19, 1977

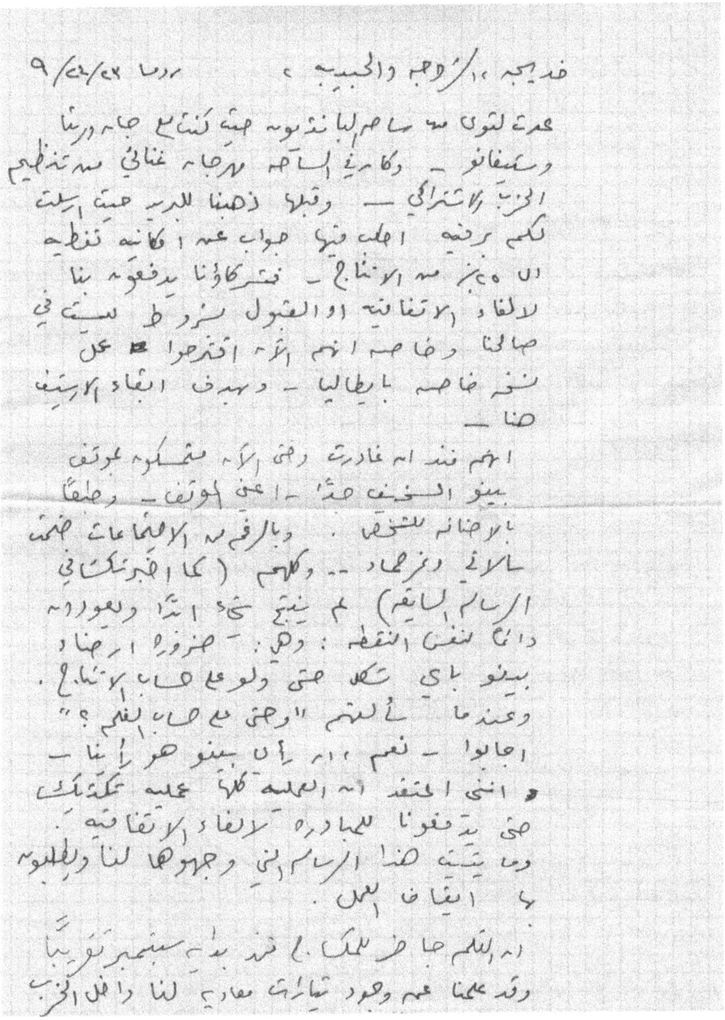

خديجة ،، الأخت والحبيبة ،   روما ٢٣/٢٤/ ٩

عدت للتو من ساحة البانثيون حيث كنت مع جان وريتا
وستيفانو — وكان في الساحة مهرجان غنائي من تنظيم
الحزب الاشتراكي —— وقبلها ذهبنا للبريد حيث إستلمت
تلكس برقية اجلت فيها جواب عن امكانية تغطية
ال ٥٠٪ من الانتاج — فشركاؤنا يدفعون بنا
لالغاء الاتفاقية او القبول بشروط ليست في
صالحنا وخاصة انهم الآن اقترحوا عمل
نسخة خاصة بإيطاليا — وبهدف الغاء الارشيف
هنا —

انهم منذ ان غادرت وحتى الآن متمسكون بموقف
بينو السخيف هذا — اعني الموقف — وطبعا
بالاضافة للشخص . وبالرغم من الاجتماعات ضمت
سالوني ودزمجاد —— وكلهم (كما اخبرتك في
الرسالة السابقة) لم ينتج شيء ابدا ولعودون
دائما لنفس النقطة : وهي : ضرورة ارضاء
بينو باي شكل حتى ولو على حساب الانتاج .
وعندما سألتهم "وحتى على حساب الفلم ؟"
اجابوا — نعم ،، ان رأي بينو هو رأينا —
انني اعتقد ان العملية كلها عملية تكتيك
حتى يدفعونا للمبادرة بالغاء الاتفاقية .
وما يثبت هذا الرسائل التي وجهوها لنا ويطلبون
بـ ايقاف العمل .

ان الفلم جاهز للمكساج فقد بدأ سبتمبر تقريبا
وقد علمنا عن وجود تيارات معادية لنا داخل الحزب

Fig. B.3 Arabic letter from Mustafa (above), September 23–24, 1977, p. 1

وبعد أن تعذر ناتوني فقد بدأ التأثير يعمل في سبيل تعطيل العمل كمرحلة
أولى والغاء الاتفاقية كمرحلة ثانية . حتى لما كان ناتوني موجوداً
فقد كان دائماً حذراً ولا يبين تأييداً كبيراً لنا خوفاً ربما
من التأثيرات الغير منطقية معنا .

ان ما تقولني عن هذا التعطيل - فقد أضعنا ٣ أسابيع
دون جدوى واعتقد بالإمكان الاستمرار بهذه المماطلة
لمدة ثلاثة شهور ... انهم في بيوتهم - والتقديرات
تفيدهم - وكلهم لهم المصالح المادية ..
لقد سمعنا في الكواليس انهم في الحقيقة ليسوا يهتمون
بهذا الانتاج ... وقد تكرر هذا القول .

بالاضافة فقد سمعنا ان البرنسيس قد تفرط - ولم
نعرف ما هي الأسباب - وعلى الأغلب سياسية

ان التعاقد قد تزعزعت الآن وخاصة بعد ان ذهب ناتوني
وبعد ان جاء (مازني) والذي سماه جاره (مزله)
أي (مذلة) - واشعر مع جاره انه حتى لو تم هذا
الاتفاق فان عدم الثقة سوف تعطل العمل في
المستقبل كالتوزيع وقضايا الايرادات وكل شيء .

اكتفي بهذا القدر - وبانتظار البرقيات -
أي تقدم وشكل الالغاء - أو التعطيل ...

أرجو أن تساعد هذه الرسالة توضيح الموقف في
الراهن ونأمل أخذ قرار بتغطية ٧٥٪
والقيام بانتاج كامل للمؤسسة . واذا لم يتخذ هذا
القرار قبل وصول هذه الرسالة -
والى اللقاء مع تحياتي

Fig. B.4 Arabic letter from Mustafa (above), September 23–24, 1977, p. 2

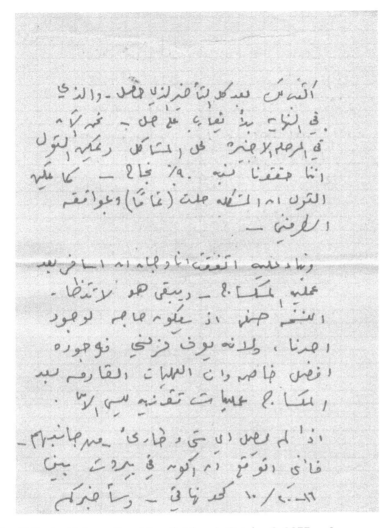

Fig. B.5 Arabic letter from Mustafa (above), October 8, 1977, p. 1

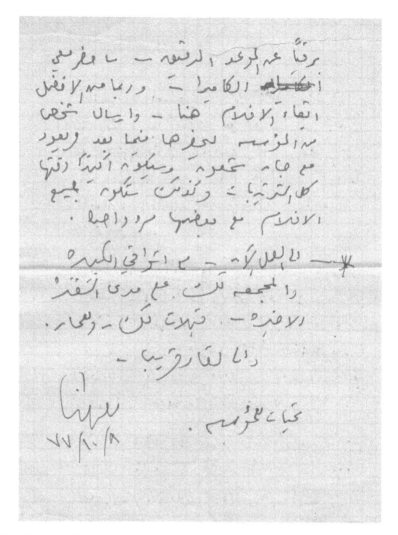

Fig. B.6 Arabic letter from Mustafa (above), October 8, 1977, p. 2

Appendix C: Filmography of Palestinian Organizations and Institutions from 1968 to 1982, and Shortly Thereafter

List of Films

The following films were produced by Palestinian organizations and institutions during the revolutionary period between 1968 and 1982, and shortly thereafter.

Films Produced by the Palestine Film Unit (PFU)/Palestinian Cinema Institution (PCI)

1. *No to a Peaceful Solution*, Black and White, 16 mm, 20 minutes, group work supervised by Mustafa Abu Ali (1969).
2. *With Soul, With Blood*, Black and White, 16 mm, 35 minutes, directed by Mustafa Abu Ali (1971).
3. *Al-Arqoub*, Black and White, 16 mm, 25 minutes, directed by Mustafa Abu Ali (1972).
4. *Zionist Aggression*, Black and White, 16 mm, 22 minutes, directed by Mustafa Abu Ali (1971).
5. *The Four-Day War*, Black and White, 16 mm, 25 minutes, directed by Samir Nimr (1972).
6. *Zionist Terrorism*, Black and White, 16 mm, 22 minutes, directed by Samir Nimr (1972).
7. *Newsreel Number 1*, Black and White, 16 mm, 22 minutes, directed by Mustafa Abu Ali (1973).

© The Author(s), under exclusive license to Springer Nature
Switzerland AG 2023
K. Habashneh, *Knights of Cinema*, Palgrave Studies in Arab
Cinema, https://doi.org/10.1007/978-3-031-18858-9

8. *Sirhan and the Pipe*, Black and White, 16 mm, 25 minutes, group work and co-production with Ezzedine Al-Jamal group (1973).

9. *They Do Not Exist*, Black and White, 16 mm, 24 minutes, directed by Mustafa Abu Ali (1974).

10. *Victory Is in Their Eyes*, Black and White, 16 mm, 35 minutes, directed by Samir Nimr (1974–1975).

11. *The Winds of Revolution*, Black and White, 16 mm, 25 minutes, directed by Samir Nimr (1974).

12. *For Whom Is the Revolution*, Black and White, 16 mm, 25 minutes, directed by Samir Nimr (1974).

13. *On the Way to Victory*, Black and White, 16 mm, 23 minutes, directed by Mustafa Abu Ali (1975).

14. *Newsreel Number 2*, Black and White, 16 mm, 21 minutes, group work supervised by Mustafa Abu Ali (1975).

15. *Newsreel Number 3*, Black and White, 16 mm, 20 minutes, group work supervised by Abdelhafeth Al-Asmar (Omar) (1977).

16. *Palestine in the Eye*, Black and White, 16 mm, 27 minutes, directed by Mustafa Abu Ali (1977).

17. *Newsreel Number 4*, Color, 16 mm, 15 minutes, group work supervised by Ibrahim Nasser (Mutee') (1977).

18. *Newsreel Number 5*, Color, 16 mm, 15 minutes, group work supervised by Mustafa Abu Ali (1978).

19. *War in Lebanon*, Black and White, 16 mm, 60 minutes, scenario by Bakir Al-Sharqawi and Samir Nimr (1977)

20. *Because Roots Don't Die*, Black and White, 16 mm, 35 minutes, directed by Nabeeha Lutfi (1977).

21. *Children of Palestine*, Color, 16 mm, 45 minutes, directed by Samir Nimr and Monica Maurer (1978).

22. *Palestinian Visions*, Color, 16 mm, 32 minutes, directed by Adnan Madanat (1977).

23. *Newsreel Number 6*, Color, 16 mm, 25 minutes, group work supervised by Mustafa Abu Ali (1978).

24. *Newsreel Number 7*, Color, 16 mm, 25 minutes, group work supervised by Mustafa Abu Ali (1979).

25. *Children Without Childhood*, Color, 16 mm, 22 minutes, directed by Khadijeh Habashneh Abu Ali (1979).

26. *The Hymn of the Free*, Color, and White, 16 mm, 25 minutes, directed by Jean Chamoun 1981.

27. *The Longest of the Days*, Black and White, 16 mm, 45 minutes, directed by Mohammad Al-Sawalmeh (1983).

28. *The Child and the Toy*, Color, 16 mm, 7 minutes, directed by Mohammad Tawfiq (Tunis) (1986).
29. *Palestinians in Lebanon After the Siege of the Camps*, Black and White, 16 mm, 30 minutes (1986).
30. *The Last Quarter*, Color, 16 mm, 10 minutes, directed by Mohammad Al-Sawalmeh (1988).

Palestinian Cinema Institution/PLO Office—Paris

1. *Martyr on the Way to Palestine*, Black and White, 16 mm, 25 minutes, directed by Ma'moun Al-Bunni, PLO Office—Paris (1975).

Palestinian Cinema Group/Palestine Research Center

1. *Scenes from the Occupation of Gaza*, Color, 16 mm, 12 minutes, directed by Mustafa Abu Ali (1973).

Films Produced with Cooperation of the Palestine Film Unit (PFU)/Palestinian Cinema Institution (PCI)

1. *Revolution Until Victory*, produced by the New York–based organization Newsreel, Black and White, 16 mm, 50 minutes, filmed in 1969–1970, completed in 1973.
2. *Testimony of Palestinian Children During Wartime* directed by Qais Al-Zubaidi produced by the Syrian General Institute of Cinema, Damascus (1973)
3. *Al-Fatah*, produced by Unitelefilm Black and White, 55 minutes, directed by Luigi Perelli (1970).
4. *Palestine, Another Vietnam*, produced by Cinema del Terzo Mondo collective, color, 16 mm, 22 minutes, directed by Jorge Denti, 1971.
5. *Palestinian Night*, co-produced between Tunisian Cinema Institute (SATPEC) and PFU, Black and White, 16 mm, 15 minutes, directed by Samir Nimr (1973).
6. *Why Do We Plant Roses ... Why Do We Carry Guns?* co-production with the German Democratic Republic Television, Color, 16 mm, 30 minutes, directed by Qasem Hawal (1974).
7. *An Oppressed People Are Always Right*, Color, 75 minutes, directed by Danish director Nils Vest (1974).
8. *Kufrshuba*, Black and white, 16 mm, 30 minutes, written by Rasmi Abu-Ali, directed by Samir Nimr, 1975.

9. *The Olive Tree*, co-produced by Vincennes Cinema Group, Black and White, 16 mm, 50 minutes, directed by Serge Le Péron, Guy Chapoullié and Jean Narboni (1975).

10. *Ici et Ailleurs [Here and Elsewhere]*, Color, 75 minutes, directed by Jean-Luc Godard (1970–1976).

11. *The Palestinian*, produced by the Revolutionary British Workers Party, Color, 16 mm, 150 minutes, directed by Roy Battersby (1977).

12. *Death in Lebanon*, co-produced by the Palestinian Popular Struggle Front, Black and White, 16 mm, 65 minutes, directed by Christian Ghazi (1981).

13. *Step by Step*, Black and White, 16 mm, 50 minutes, directed by Randa Chahal (1977).

14. *Ezzedine Qalaq*, produced by Vincennes Cinema Group, Black and White, 16 mm, 60 minutes, directed by Serge Le Peron and Guy Chapoullié (1979).

15. *The Palestine Red Crescent Society*, produced by the Palestinian Red Crescent Society, Color, 16 mm, 45 minutes, directed by Monica Maurer and Samir Nimr (1979).

16. *The Fifth War*, produced by PCI and Samed Cinema production in cooperation with the German Democratic Republic, Color, 16 mm, 30 minutes, directed by Monica Maurer and Samir Nimr (1980).

17. *Eyes of the Nation*, Black and White, 55 minutes, produced by the Vietnamese Institute for Documentary and News (1981).

18. *Born Out of Death*, co-produced by the Unified Information Office, Color, 16 mm, 9 minutes, directed by Monica Maurer (1981).

19. *Path to the Land*, produced with the Cuban Cinema Institute, Color, 16 mm, 50 minutes in two parts (1982).

20. *Under the Rubble,* produced with a Lebanese Group, Black and White, 16 mm, 55 minutes, directed by Jean Chamoun and Mai Masri (1983).

Department of Culture and Information (Culture and Arts Division)/PLO

1. *Youth Camps*, Black and White, 16 mm, 15 minutes, directed by Ismael Shamout (1972).

2. *Urgent Call,* Black and White, 16 mm, 5 minutes, directed by Ismail Shammout (1973).

3. *Memories and Fire*, 16 mm, 11 minutes, directed by Ismail Shammout (1973).

4. *On the Path to Palestine,* Black and White, 16 mm, 27 minutes, directed by Ismail Shammout (1972).
5. *A Voice from Jerusalem,* Color, 35 mm, 20 minutes, directed by Qais Al-Zubaidi (1977).
6. *Counter Siege,* Color, 35 mm, 22 minutes, directed by Qais Al-Zubaidi (1978).
7. *Homeland of Barbed Wire,* Color, 16 mm, 60 minutes, directed by Qais Al-Zubaidi (1980).
8. *Palestine: A Peoples' Record,* Black and White, 35 mm, 110 minutes, directed by Qais Al-Zubaidi (1982).
9. *Abu Salma,* Color, 16 mm, 45 minutes, directed by Yahya Barakat (1982).
10. *Ever in the Memory,* Color, 16 mm, 27 minutes, directed by Hikmat Daoud, Damascus (1982).
11. *Confrontation,* Color, 16 mm, 28 minutes, directed by Qais Al-Zubaidi (1983).
12. *Umm Ali,* Color, 16 mm, 20 minutes, directed by Mohammad Tawfeq (1983).
13. *File of a Massacre,* Color, 16 mm, 34 minutes, directed by Qais Al-Zubaidi (1984).
14. *Identity,* Color, 16 mm, 45 minutes, directed by Qasem Hawal (1984).
15. *Path to Palestine* (cartoon), Color, 16 mm, 8 minutes, directed by Layal Badr, Damascus (1985).
16. *Al-Natour,* Color, 35 mm, 26 minutes, directed by Mohammad Tawfeq, Tunis (1988).
17. *Shared Days,* Color, Betacam, 45 minutes, directed by Yahya Barakat, Tunis (1989).
18. *Question Mark* (cartoon), Color, 16 mm, 4 minutes, directed by Jamal Shammout (1990).
19. *The Upper Gate,* Color, 16 mm, 90 minutes, directed by Arab Lutfi, Tunis (1990).
20. *Rimal Al-Sawafi,* Color, Betacam, 45 minutes, directed by Yahya Barakat, Tunis (1991).

The department also produced three historical fiction TV series: *With My Own Eyes* about the memoir of the attorney Felicia Langer, directed by Saleem Musa (1979); *Ezzedine Al-Qassam,* directed by Haitham Haqqi (1981); and *Bir Al-Shoum,* based on a novel by Faisal Hourani, directed by Qais Al-Zubaidi (1982).

Central Information/Artistic Section/Popular Front for the Liberation of Palestine

1. *On the Path of the Palestinian Revolution*, Black and White, 16 mm, 33 minutes, directed by Fouad Zantout, Beirut (1970).
2. *Al-Nahr Al-Bared*, Black and White, 16 mm, 15 minutes, directed by Qasem Hawal, Beirut (1971).
3. *The Word as a Gun: Ghassan Kanafani*, Black and white, 16 mm, 20 minutes, directed by Qasem Hawal, Beirut (1972).
4. *The Guns Will Not Fall*, Black and white, 16 mm, 17 minutes, directed by Qasem Hawal, Beirut (1973).
5. *Our Small Houses*, Black and white, 16 mm, 24 minutes, directed by Qasem Hawal, Beirut (1974).
6. *Lebanon—Tal Al-Za'atar*, Black and White, 16 mm, 20 minutes, directed by Qasem Hawal, Beirut (1978).
7. *Al-Hadaf News Reel No One*, Black and White, 16 mm, 15 minutes, supervised by Fouad Zantout, Beirut (1979).
8. *Black Papers*, Black and White, 16 mm, 20 minutes, written and edited by Fouad Zantout, Beirut (1979).
9. *The Betrayal*, Color, 16 mm, 20 minutes, written and edited by Fouad Zantout, Beirut (1980).
10. *Return to Haifa*, a feature-length fiction film based on Ghassan Kanafani's novel, Color, 35 mm, 74 minutes, directed by Qasem Hawal, produced by The Land Institute for Cinema Production (1981).
11. *Good Morning Beirut*, Color, 16 mm, 23 minutes, directed by Jabreel 'Awad, Damascus (1983).

Artistic Committee/Democratic Front for the Liberation of Palestine

1. *One Hundred Faces for a Single Day*, Black and White, 35 mm, 85 minutes, directed by Christian Ghazi, co-produced by the General Cinema Institute, Damascus (1972).
2. *The Path*, Black and White, 16 mm, 15 minutes, directed by Rafeq Hajjar, Beirut (1972).
3. *The Guns Are United*, Black and White, 16 mm, 30 minutes, directed by Rafeq Hajjar, Beirut (1973).

4. *Palestinian May*, Black and White, 16 mm, 44 minutes, directed by Rafeq Hajjar and Sufian Al-Ramahi, Beirut (1974).
5. *Al-Intifadah*, Black and White, 16 mm, 16 minutes, directed by Rafeq Hajjar, Beirut (1975).
6. *Born in Palestine*, Black and White, 35 mm, 30 minutes, directed by Rafeq Hajjar, co-produced by the German Democratic Republic, Beirut (1975).
7. *News from Tal Al-Za'atar*, Color, 16 mm, 15 minutes, directed by Adnan Madanat, Beirut (1976).
8. *The Road to Surrender*, Black and White, 16 mm, 15 minutes, directed by Mohammad Tawfiq, Beirut (1981).

SAMED Institute

1. *The Key*, Color, 16 mm, 30 minutes, directed by Ghaleb Sha'ath, Beirut (1976).
2. *Land Day*, Color, 16 mm, 38 minutes, directed by Ghaleb Sha'ath, Beirut (1978).
3. *Olive Branch*, Color, 16 mm, 20 minutes, directed by Ghaleb Sha'ath, Beirut (1981).

Palestinian Popular Struggle Front (Beirut)

1. *Death in Lebanon*, Black and White, 16 mm, 65 minutes, directed by Christian Ghazi, co-produced with the Palestinian Cinema Institution, Beirut (1981).
2. *Journey of a Struggle*, Color, 16 mm, 30 minutes, directed by Yahya Barakat, Beirut (1981).

General Command, Popular Front for the Liberation of Palestine

The General Command of the Popular Front for the Liberation of Palestine filmed the following color material for three 16 mm documentary films in 1974:

- Footage of Al-Khalsa Operation before they headed to the fedayee operation.

- Footage of the Bissan Operation before they headed to the fedayee operation.
- A graduation of fighters from one of the front's bases.

After adding audio to the footage, three documentary films were produced about the Al-Khalsa Operation, the Al-Bissan Operation, and the graduation of fighters from one of the front's bases, built on interviews with the fighters of Al-Khalsa operation before they were martyred in 1974, and on the scenes of graduation of one of the front's military cohorts. The General Command of the PFLP did not have a cinema department or office.[1]

Arabic Liberation Front

- *Mountain of Sacrifice and Steadfastness*, 16 mm, 18 minutes, directed by Ibrahim Sammour, 1977.[2]

---

[1] Hassan Abu Ghanimeh, *Palestine in the Cinematic Eye*, Damascus: Arab Writers Union, 1981, p. 335.

[2] Qais Al- Zubaidi, *Palestine in Cinema*, Beirut: Institute for Palestine Studies, 2006, p. 106. This is a directory of 800 films and is different from the Chmait/Hennebelle book of the same title, *Palestine in Cinema*, republished by the Palestinian Ministry of Culture, in 2006.

Appendix D: Palestinian Films and Film Footage in the Tunisian Film Archive

List of Palestinian Films and Film Footage Available at the Tunisian Film Archive

Number	Title	Production	Number of segments	Audio	Size (mm)
1	*From the East, The Time of War*	Palestinian Liberation Organization	2	Arabic	16
2	*Events in Lebanon*	Palestinian Liberation Organization	3	Arabic	16
3	*With Soul, With Blood*	Palestinian Liberation Organization	1	Arabic	16
4	*Newsreel Number 2*	Palestinian Liberation Organization	1	Arabic	16
5	*They Do Not Exist*	Palestinian Liberation Organization	1	Arabic	16
6	*Palestine in the Eye*	Palestinian Liberation Organization	1	Arabic	16
7	*Because Roots Don't Die (Tal Al-Za'atar)*	Palestinian Liberation Organization	3	Arabic	16
8	*The Child and The Toy*	Palestinian Liberation Organization	1	Arabic	16
9	*Nobel Prize*	Palestinian Liberation Organization	1	Arabic, French, English	35

(continued)

© The Author(s), under exclusive license to Springer Nature Switzerland AG 2023
K. Habashneh, *Knights of Cinema*, Palgrave Studies in Arab Cinema, https://doi.org/10.1007/978-3-031-18858-9

(continued)

Number	Title	Production	Number of segments	Audio	Size (mm)
10	Palestinian National Council	Palestinian Liberation Organization	Unknown	Arabic	16
11	Israeli Prisoners	Palestinian Liberation Organization	Unknown	Arabic	16
12	Um Ali	Palestinian Liberation Organization	1	French, English	16
13	In a Bad Time	Palestinian Liberation Organization	1	French, English	16
14	The Longest of the Days	Palestinian Liberation Organization	1	Arabic	16
15	Violence in String	Palestinian Liberation Organization	1	Arabic	16
16	The Intifada (The Last Quarter)	Palestinian Liberation Organization	2	Arabic	35
17	Western Withdrawal	Palestinian Liberation Organization	1	Arabic	16
18	Roots of Life	Palestinian Liberation Organization	1	Arabic	16
19	The Conspiracy	Palestinian Liberation Organization	1	Arabic	16
20	The Middle East	Palestinian Liberation Organization	5	Arabic	16
21	Zionism	Palestinian Liberation Organization	7	Arabic	16
22	Accused of Genocide	Palestinian Liberation Organization	1	Arabic	16
23	Beirut	Palestinian Liberation Organization	1	Arabic	16
24	Jerusalem	Palestinian Liberation Organization	1	Arabic	16
25	The Seventeenth Round	Palestinian Liberation Organization	Unknown		16
26	Abu Al-Qasem Al-Natour	Palestinian Liberation Organization	2	Arabic	35
27	Sayidah	Palestinian Liberation Organization	4	Arabic	16

Appendix E: Biographies of the Founders of the Palestine Film Unit/Palestinian Cinema Institution

Sulafa Jadallah

- Born in Nablus in 1941.
- Completed her primary and secondary education at Al-Aishiyyeh School in Nablus.
- Developed her skills in photography with her brother Rima' at the beginning of the 1950s, and together they established an association for youth interested in all forms of art.
- Graduated from the Higher Institute of Cinema in Cairo, 1964, with high merit. She was the first female Arab cinematographer.
- Worked as a cinematographer in the cinema department of the Ministry of Information in Jordan at the end of 1965.
- Filmed the Jordanian Newsreel and continued filming with Hani Jawharieh during the events of the 1967 war.
- Joined the Fatah movement of the Palestinian Revolution in 1967, and started filming the militants, fighters, and martyrs, with her personal equipment, developing the images at home.

K. Habashneh, *Knights of Cinema*, Palgrave Studies in Arab Cinema, https://doi.org/10.1007/978-3-031-18858-9

- Contributed in producing footage for a number of films during her work at the Ministry of Information, including *The Exodus* (1967) and *The Scorched Earth* in (1968), both directed by Ali Siyam. She also contributed to the film *The Palestinian Right* directed by Mustafa Abu Ali in 1968.
- Established the Palestine Film Unit with Hani Jawharieh and Mustafa Abu Ali in 1968.
- Resigned from the Ministry of Information at the beginning of 1969 to dedicate all her working time for the photography department, and the newly established Palestine Film Unit.
- Became injured in the head in 1969 which left her half paralyzed and prevented her from continuing her work as a cinematographer.
- Returned to work with the Palestine Film Unit/Palestinian Cinema Institution in 1975–1976, at the encouragement of Hani Jawharieh.
- Worked with Hani on organizing the administration at the institute, training new personnel, and developing the work of the filmmakers in general.
- Unable to continue the work following the martyrdom of Hani, Mutee', and Omar, she moved to Damascus to live with her siblings.
- Died in 2002 in Damascus, where she spent her last days.
- Remains the pioneering filmmaker who documented the events and activities of the Palestinian Revolution since 1967.

THE MARTYR HANI JAWHARIEH (1939–1976)

- Born in Jerusalem in 1939.
- Completed his secondary studies at the Bishop's School in Jerusalem in 1957.
- Studied filmmaking for one year at the Higher Institute of Cinema in Cairo from 1962 to 1963.
- Received a scholarship from the Jordanian Ministry of Information in 1964 to study cinematography at the London School of Film Technique (later called the London Film School).
- Graduated in mid-1966 and worked in the cinema department of the Jordanian Ministry of Information.
- Met Sulafa Jadallah, who worked as a cinematographer at the cinema department of the Ministry of Information. Together, they filmed the aftermath of the June 1967 War, and the large exodus of Palestinians from the King Hussein Bridge (Allenby Bridge).

- Filmed for the Newsreel that was directed by the head of the department, Ali Siyam.
- Joined, in mid-1967, the Fatah Information Office with his friend Mustafa Abu Ali and Sulafa Jadallah and established the photography department.
- Initiated with his colleagues the Palestine Film Unit, at the end of 1968, to document the activities of the revolution using a borrowed camera.
- They produced the PFU's first film *No to a Peaceful Solution* at the end of 1969, about the Palestinian people's and revolution's leaders' objection to the Rogers Plan.
- Resigned from the cinema department of the Ministry of Information to dedicate his work to the photography department, and the newly established Palestine Film Unit with Sulafa Jadallah and Mustafa Abu Ali.
- Accompanied Mustafa Abu Ali, during the events of Black September in 1970, in shooting documentary footage that Mustafa later used for the film *With Soul, With Blood* about Black September.
- Remained in Jordan until October 1975 when he was able to rejoin the revolutionary forces in Beirut, when the Palestine Film Unit had evolved into the Palestinian Cinema Institution.
- Became the Director Deputy of the Palestinian Cinema Institution.
- Martyred on April 11, 1976, as he filmed the battles waged by the Palestinian revolution and the joint Lebanese forces against the Separatist Lebanese forces that were aligned with Israel at Aintoura mountain.
- Worked on several films throughout his life, including:

  - *Exodus* (1967), *The Scorched Earth* (1968), *Zahrat Al Mada'en* (1969), *The Bridge of Return* (1969), directed by Ali Siyam and produced by the cinema department of the Jordanian Ministry of Information
  - *The Palestinian Right* (1968), directed by Mustafa Abu Ali, produced by the Jordanian Ministry of Information
  - *Testimony of Palestinian Children During Wartime* (1969), directed by Qais Al-Zubaidi, co-produced by the Palestine Film Unit and the Syrian General Cinema Organization

- *No to a Peaceful Solution* (1969), *With Soul, With Blood* (1971), *Newsreel Number 2* (1975), *On the Path to Victory* (1975), directed by Mustafa Abu Ali and produced by the Palestine Film Unit/ Palestinian Cinema Institution.
- *The Key* in 1976, directed by Ghaleb Sha'at, produced by the cinema department of SAMED.

MUSTAFA ABU ALI

- Born in Al-Malha, district of Jerusalem in 1940.
- Completed his secondary education at the Al-Hussein College in Amman, received his matric certificate with honors in 1957, and was awarded a scholarship to study for a year at the American University of Beirut.
- Completed three years of study at the architecture faculty at the University of California at Berkeley, in the United States, 1961–1964.
- Received a diploma in cinema from the London School of Film Technique in 1967 (later known as the London Film School).
- Worked as a film director in the cinema department of the Jordanian Ministry of Information and the Jordan Television between 1967 and 1970.
- Held a number of positions, notably the following:

  - Director of the Palestine Film Unit/Palestinian Cinema Institution in Beirut from 1971 to 1982.
  - Secretary of the Palestinian Cinema Group of the Palestine Research Center (for which he was voted) in Beirut in November, 1972, upon return from the Carthage Days of Cinema festival.
  - Member of the Union for Arab Broadcasting (for which he was voted) in 1974.

- Wrote a book entitled *About Palestinian Cinema* with the film critic Hassan Abu Ghanimeh in 1975.
- Managed and oversaw the *Palestinian Image* magazine published by the Palestinian Cinema Institution—Beirut, in 1978–1979.
- Contributed to developing documentary films on Palestine produced in Beirut from 1971 to 1980. The production teams came from Germany, France, Britain, Sweden, Denmark, Italy, the Soviet Union, Egypt, Brazil, and Greece.

- Wrote and directed thirty documentary films and one short fiction film based on the story *Abbas and Deek Al Hajal* by Tawfiq Zayyad, produced by the Jordan Television.
- Wrote scripts for four feature-length fiction films including:

  - *Days of Love and Death*, adapted from a novel by Rashad Abu Shawar in 1973.
  - *The Pessoptimist*, adapted from a novel by Emile Habibi entitled *The Secret Life of Saeed: The Pessoptimist*.
  - *Awaiting Peace*, original script, 2002.
  - *The Stranger*, original script, 2004.

- Established and headed Bissan Films in Amman in 1984 and in Ramallah from 1999 to 2009
- Re-established the Palestinian Cinema Group in Ramallah in 2004.
- Served as a member of the jury at the first Al-Jazeera International Film Festival in 2006.
- Earned fourteen prizes at international cinema festivals.
- Received a golden achievement award for all his work at the Seventh Ismailia International Film Festival in Egypt in 2003.
- Died on July 30, 2009, and was buried in Ramallah.

Appendix F: Covers and Table of Contents of the Palestinian Image magazine

Fig. F.1 Front cover of the *Palestinian Image* magazine, First Issue, November 1978

© The Author(s), under exclusive license to Springer Nature
Switzerland AG 2023
K. Habashneh, *Knights of Cinema*, Palgrave Studies in Arab
Cinema, https://doi.org/10.1007/978-3-031-18858-9

Fig. F.2 Corresponding table of contents to *Palestinian Image* magazine, First Issue, November 1978

Translation of (Figs. F.1 and F.2)

The Palestinian Image, Quarterly Issue, by Palestinian Cinema Institution

Unified Information, Palestine Liberation Organization

First Issue, 1978

Issue Title: The End of an Era and the Beginning of Another by the Palestinian Cinema Institution

"Palestinian Cinema exists" by Serge Le Peron

"For a lively film about Palestine": An Interview with Omar Al-Mukhtar

"Palestine Exists" by Ezzeddine Qalaq

"Snapshots from the cinematographic experience during the war" by Mustafa Abu Ali

News

Documents:

- Films that gained the awards of Palestinian Liberation Movement
- Foreign films about the Palestinian Cause
- A list of Palestinian films

Translation of (Figs. F.3 and F.4)

The Image, Quarterly Issue, by Palestinian Cinema Institution, Unified Information, Palestine Liberation Organization

Second Issue, March 1979

Under supervision of Adnan Madanat, Mustafa Abu Ali, Jean Chamoun

Issue Title: Towards a Palestinian Cinema Unity

"An Opinion: National parties and National cinema" by A.M.

"Papers for memory: Hani Jawharieh as a photographer" by Mustafa Abu Ali

"Snapshots from the practical experience" by Adnan Madanat

"In Zionist cinema: About the film *We are Arab Jews in Israel*" by Jean Chamoun

"A study: *The Search for a Popular Cinema*" by Jorge Sanjines, translated by Kh.A.A.

"From the experiences of the Palestinian Cinema Institution: Cinematographic screenings and their beginnings" by Khadijeh Abu Ali

"Festivals: Palestinian cinema in Carthage and Leipzig" by A.M.

About the Palestinian cinema: Opinions on *Tal Al-Za'atar* film.

A new film: *The Palestinian Rights in Life*

News

Documents:

- Arab cinematographers' statement at the festival of Carthage
- Letters between the film censorship council, the theaters in Israel, and Mario Ogenberg

Awards

Fig. F.3   Front cover of the *Palestinian Image* magazine, Second Issue, March 1979

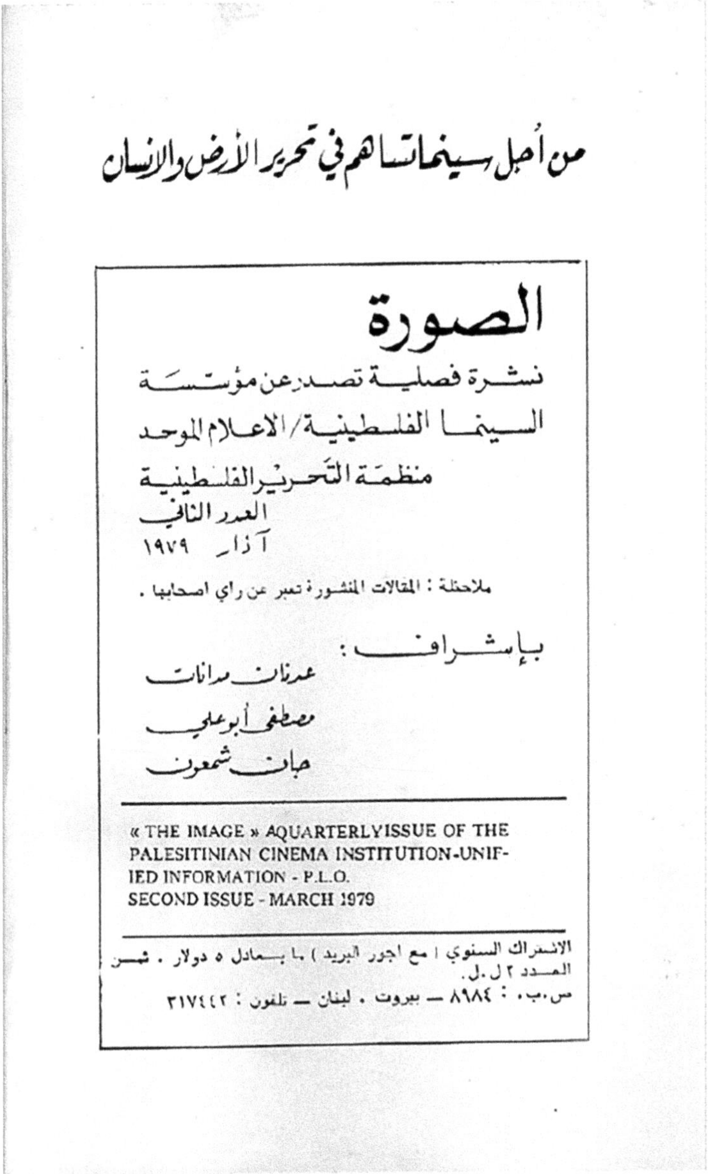

من أجل سينماتساهم في تحرير الأرض والإنسان

الصورة

نشــرة فصليــة تصــدر عن مؤســسة
الســينــا الفلــسطينيــة / الاعــلام الموحد
منظمة التَحــريــر الفلــسطينية
العدد الثاني
آزار ١٩٧٩

ملاحظة : المقالات المنشورة تعبر عن رأي أصحابها .

بإشــراف :
عدنان مدانات
مصطفى أبوعلي
حبان شمعون

« THE IMAGE » A QUARTERLY ISSUE OF THE
PALESITINIAN CINEMA INSTITUTION-UNIF-
IED INFORMATION - P.L.O.
SECOND ISSUE - MARCH 1979

الاشتراك السنوي (مع أجور البريد) بـا يــعادل ٥ دولار . ثمـر
الـعـــدد ٢ ل.ل.
ص.ب. : ٨٩٨٤ — بيروت . لبنان — تلفون : ٢١٧٤٤٢

Fig. F.4 Corresponding table of contents to *Palestinian Image* magazine, Second Issue, March 1979

(Figs. F.5 and F.6)
English translation for Fig. F.5 is provided in Fig. F.6.

Fig. F.5   Front cover of the *Palestinian Image* magazine, Third Issue, 1979

« THE IMAGE » A QUARTERLY ISSUE OF THE
PALESTINIAN CINEMA INSTITUTION - UNIFIED
INFORMATION - P.L.O.
THIRD ISSUE — JUNE — 1979

Fig. F.6 Corresponding table of contents to *Palestinian Image* magazine, Third Issue, 1979

Fig. F.7 Front cover of the *Palestinian Image* magazine Fourth Issue, November 1979

(Fig. F.8)

The Image, A Quarterly Issue, Palestinian Cinema Institution, Unified Information, Palestine Liberation Organization

Fourth Issue, November 1979

Under supervision of Mustafa Abu Ali

Issue title: The Image

"Primal planning of what cinema is?" by Qais Al-Zubaidi

"About materialistic reading of cinema" by Jean-Patrick Loubel

"Cinema: art, knowledge, and attitude" by Nabil Al Maleh

"Zionist cinema, settlement, and oppression culture" by Alan Zaef

"With the director Abed El Aziz Al Tulbi" by Amer Hassan Bader

"The social condition and artistic culture" by Dr. Faisal Darraj

"About the popular art concept" by Adnan Madanat

The revolution and culture file: Yihya Yakhlof, Faisal Hourani, Muhammad Ismail, Adnan Madanat

"Creative Solidarity" by Eduardo Mana

"Why do I draw?" by Burhan Karkoutli

"Critical comments on the fine arts Palestinian movement" by Muna Al-Saudi

"Palestinian children's paintings" by M. S.

Documents

The earth group for theater and music

News

Fig. F.8 Corresponding table of contents to *Palestinian Image* magazine, Fourth Issue, November 1979

Appendix G: Photographs Documenting the Palestine Film Unit and Palestinian Cinema Institution

(Figs. G.1, G.2, G.3, G.4, G.5, G.6, G.7, G.8, G.9, G.10, G.11, G.12, G.13, G.14, G.15, G.16, G.17, G.18, G.19, G.20, G.21, G.22, G.23, G.24, G.25, G.26 and G.27)

Fig. G.1 Mustafa and Hani (back to the camera) with the fighters at the fedayee bases (Al-Karameh Ghor), 1969

Fig. G.2 Hassan Abu Ghanimeh speaks during a symposium at the Baghdad International Festival for Films and TV Programs on Palestine, 1973. Mustafa sits next to him. Palestinian novelist Jabra Ibrahim Jabra to the left of Abu Ghanimeh

Fig. G.3 The Palestinian delegation at a meeting for the Union of Arab Documentarists at the Leipzig Festival, 1974. The poet Ezzedine Al-Manasra is sitting in the middle; to the right are Mutee' and Rafiq Hajjar, and to the left the Syrian director Omar Amiralay and Qasem Hawal

Fig. G.4 The cover of *Palestine the Revolution* (*Falastin Al-Thawra*) issue which includes a special feature on the martyr Hani Jawharieh, April 1976

Fig. G.5 Hani Jawharieh prize awarded by the Palestinian Cinema Institution at Arab and International festivals in recognition of best militant films

Fig. G.6 Hind Jawharieh and Ghassan Matar announce the Hani Jawharieh prize, in Carthage Days of Cinema Festival, 1978

Fig. G.7 Mustafa (at the left) speaks with the Palestinian novelist Tawfiq Fayyad, and on the right are the poet Ezzedine Al-Manasrah and the director Ghaleb Sha'ath, 1976

Fig. G.8 Mustafa talks to Ghassan Matar while filming an interview with Um Karoum from Tal Al-Za'atar, 1976

Fig. G.9 Director Randa Chahal interviews a woman fleeing Tal Al-Za'atar after the fall of the camp, August 1976

Fig. G.10   Omar Al-Mukhtar films during the war in Lebanon, 1976–1977

Fig. G.11 Director Adnan Madanat stands behind Omar Al-Mukhtar who is standing next to the sound engineer Mohammad 'Awad while filming *Palestinian Visions*, 1977

Fig. G.12 The photographers from the right: 'Azzam 'Alawan, Yousef Al-Qutob, Khalil Sa'adeh, 1977

Fig. G.13 Abu Nidal (Nazeh) speaking with Faisal Daraj and Mustafa Abu Ali as they await the screening of the film *Tal Al-Za'atar*, 1978. Behind Mustafa sits the director Yahya Barakat

Fig. G.14 From right, Lebanese editor and director Fouad Zantout, Abu Nidal Mustafa Abu Ali, and Jean Chamoun await the screening of the film *Tal Al-Za'atar*, 1978

Fig. G.15 The cover of *Palestine of the Revolution* (*Falastin Al-Thawra*) with the martyrs Ibrahim Naser (Mutee') and Abdelhafiz Al-Asmar (Omar Al-Mukhtar), March 1978

Fig. G.16 A commemorative shot of the photographer Marwan Salameh and sound engineer Shaher Al-Soumi with the fighters, 1977

Fig. G.17 British actress Vanessa Redgrave with the fighters after filming, 1978

Fig. G.18 Director Khadijeh Abu Ali Habashneh with the filmmaker Samir Nimr while filming *Children Without Childhood*, 1979

Fig. G.19 Khadijeh and Mustafa at Carthage Days of Cinema Festival—Tunis, 1980

Fig. G.20 Lebanese director Jean Chamoun with Samir Nimr while filming in Beirut, 1980

السادة / ادارة ستوديو بعلبك

تحية طيبة وبعد ،

ترجو مؤسسة السينما الفلسطينية (الاعلام الموحد) ان يوقف
العمل بطباعة الافلام على حساب الطلبات القديمة وارسال نيجاتيف
الافلام التالية – ليس لهم وجود – مشاهد من الاحتلال نسي فنزة –
كسر شوبا – على طريق النصر – شورة حتى النصر – عدوان صهيوني –
بالروح بالدم – الجريدة العدد الاول – الجريدة العدد الثاني –
الفتح – سرحان – فلسطين ستنتصر – حرب الايام الاربعة – رياح
التحرير – لمن الثورة .

وذلك كي يتسنى لنا طلب افلام جديدة على حسب خطة
عملنا لسنة ١٩٧٦ .

مع وافر شكرنا وتقديرنا . كما يرجى تزويدنا بجميع الفواتير
المطلوبة منا حتى هذا التاريخ لتسديدها فورا .

مؤسسة السينما الفلسطينية

١٩٧٦/٣/٢٤

Fig. G.21   A letter from the Palestinian Cinema Institution to Studio Ba'albak asking them to stop printing copies of their films, and to return the 15 film negatives kept at the studio

Fig. G.22   A poster for the Palestinian Cinema Institution

Fig. G.23   A PCI poster commemorating the tenth anniversary of the PFU

Fig. G.24   Film guide by the Palestinian Cinema Institution

Fig. G.25   A poster of the Palestine Cinema Week in Switzerland, 1976

Fig. G.26 A poster of the Palestine Cinema Week in Rabat, Morocco May 1978

Fig. G.27   Poster of the PCI Newsreel

BIBLIOGRAPHY

CHAPTER 1

Chmait, Walid and Guy Hennebelle, eds. *Filastin fi al-Sinima [Palestine in Cinema]*, 2nd ed. Ramallah: Wizarat al-Thaqafah al-Filastiniyah, al-Hay'ah al-'Ammah al-Filastiniyah lil Kitab, 2006.

Al-Najjar, Tayseer. Interview with Mustafa Abu Ali. Source uncertain, possibly *Al Arab Al Yaum* in Jordan, date NA, possibly late 1990s.

Al-Shayeb, Yousef. Interview with Mustafa Abu Ali. *Al-Ayyam* newspaper, August 4, 2009.

Interview with Mustafa Abu Ali's siblings conducted by the author on July 25th, 2018.

Interview with Rasmi Abu Ali conducted by the author, June 26th, 2019.

Interview with Samir Faraj conducted by the author on May 20th, 2018.

Interview with Abdelraheem Jadallah, presented in a letter obtained at the request of the author on February 27th, 2018.

Interview with Hind Jawharieh's (Janette Fattaleh) conducted by the author October 25th, 2017.

Interview with Riyad Jawharieh conducted by the author on October 16th, 2016.

Interview with Riyad Jawharieh conducted by the author on October 25th, 2016.

CHAPTER 2

Interview with Enaya Abu Awn conducted by the author at Sep 28th, 2017.

Interview with Naseef (Adil al Kesbeh) conducted by the author on June 27th, 2014.

© The Author(s), under exclusive license to Springer Nature Switzerland AG 2023
K. Habashneh, *Knights of Cinema*, Palgrave Studies in Arab Cinema, https://doi.org/10.1007/978-3-031-18858-9

Interview with Abdelraheem Jadallah conducted by the author on February 27th, 2018.

Interview with Eram Jadallah conducted by the author on June 23rd, 2018.

Interview with Nabil Mahdi conducted by the author on June 20, 2017.

Interview with Amneh Naser conducted by the author on September 24th, 2017.

Interview with Abu Thareef conducted by the author on August 15th, 2016.

CHAPTER 3

Abu Ghanimeh, Hassan. *Filastin wa-al'Ayn al-Sinima'I [Palestine and the Cinematic Eye]*. Damascus: Ittihad al-Kuttab al-'Arab, 1981.

Abu Ali, Mustafa and Hassan Abu Ghanimeh. *An al-Sinima al-Filastiniyah [About the Palestinian Cinema]*. Beirut: Wihdet Aflam Filastin /Muassaset al-Sinima al-Filastiniyah, 1975.

Chmait, Walid and Guy Hennebelle, eds. *Filastin fi al-Sinima [Palestine in Cinema]*, 2nd ed. Ramallah: Wizarat al-Thaqafah al-Filastiniyah, al-Hay'ah al-'Ammah al-Filastiniyah lil Kitab, 2006.

Al-Najjar, Tayseer. Interview with Mustafa Abu Ali. Source uncertain, possibly *Al Arab Al Yaum* in Jordan, date NA, possibly late 1990s.

Interview with Salah Abu Hannoud conducted by the author on September 25th, 2015.

Interview with Hind Jawharieh conducted by the author on October 15th, 2017.

Interview with Naseef conducted by the author on June 27th, 2014.

Interview with Amneh Naser conducted by the author on September 24th, 2017.

Interview with Abu Thareef conducted by the author on August 15th, 2016.

Interview with Elias Sanbar, conducted by the author in Paris, March 12, 2018

CHAPTER 4

Abu Ali, Khadijeh. "Al-'Arud al- Sinima'iyah wa Bidayatuha" ["Film Screenings and their Beginnings"]. *Al-Surah al-Filastiniyah [Palestinian Image]*. Second issue, March 1979, Beirut: Muassaset al-Sinima al-Filastiniyah, p. 31-35.

Abu Ali, Mustafa and Hassan Abu Ghanimeh. *An al-Sinima al-Filastiniyah [About the Palestinian Cinema]*. Beirut: Wihdet Aflam Filastin /Muassaset al-Sinima al-Filastiniyah, 1975.

Abu Ghanimeh, Hassan. *Filastin wa-al'Ayn al-Sinima'I [Palestine and the Cinematic Eye]*. Damascus: Ittihad al-Kuttab al-'Arab, 1981.

Chmait, Walid and Guy Hennebelle, eds. *Filastin fi al-Sinima [Palestine in Cinema]*, 2nd ed. Ramallah: Wizarat al-Thaqafah al-Filastiniyah, al-Hay'ah al-'Ammah al-Filastiniyah lil Kitab, 2006.

Oudat, Husayn al-. *Al-Sinima wa-al Qadiyah al-Filastiniyah [Cinema and the Palestinian Cause]*. Damascus: Al-Ahali. 1987

Robledo, Pablo. *Montoneros Y Palestina: De la Revolution a La Dictadura [Montoneros and Palestine: From Revolution to Dictatorship]*. Buenos Aires: Editorial Planeta, 2018.

Interview with Naseef conducted on June 27th, 2014.

Interview with Abu Thareef conducted on August 15th, 2016.

Interview with 'Amneh Naser conducted on September 24th, 2017.

Interview with Nabil conducted on September 27th, 2017.

Interview with Mahmoud Nofal, conducted on October 17th, 2017.

Interview with Nazeh Abu Nidal conducted on November 15, 2018.

Interview with Sahar Abu Ghanimeh conducted by the author on October 17th, 2017.

CHAPTER 5

Abu Ali, Mustafa. "Shaheed al-Sinima al-Nidaliyah" ["The Martyr of the Militant Cinema"]. *Al-Surah al-Filastiniyah [Palestinian Image]*, First issue, November 1978, Beirut: Muassaset al-Sinima al-Filastiniyah p. 16-17.

Abu Ali, Mustafa. "Laqatat min al-Tajribah al-Sinima'iyah fi al-Harab al-Lubnaniyah (1975-1976)" ["Snapshots of the Cinematic Experience During the Lebanese War (1975-1976)". *Al-Surah al-Filastiniyah [Palestinian Image]*, First issue, 1978, Beirut: Muassaset al-Sinima al-Filastiniyah, p.15-19.

Abu Ali, Mustafa. "Hani ka Musawer" ["Hani as Cinematographer"]. *Al-Surah al-Filastiniyah [Palestinian Image]*, Second issue, November 1979, Beirut: Muassaset al-Sinima al-Filastiniyah, p. 9-14.

Abu Ghanimeh, Hassan. *Filastin wa-al'Ayn al-Sinima'I [Palestine and the Cinematic Eye]*. Damascus: Ittihad al-Kuttab al-'Arab, 1981.

Chmait, Walid and Guy Hennebelle, eds. *Filastin fi al-Sinima [Palestine in Cinema]*, 2nd ed. Ramallah: Wizarat al-Thaqafah al-Filastiniyah, al-Hay'ah al-'Ammah al-Filastiniyah lil Kitab, 2006.

"Nihnu fi al-Asl Muqatilun" ["We Are Originally Militants"], interview with cinematographer Omar Al-Mukhtar, *Al-Surah al-Filastiniyah [Palestinian Image]*. First issue, 1978, Beirut: Muassaset al-Sinima al-Filastiniyah, p. 9-10. (Author NA)

CHAPTER 6

Abu Ali, Mustafa. "Laqatat min al-Tajribah al-Sinima'iyah fi al-Harab al-Lubnaniyah (1975-1976)" ["Snapshots of the Cinematic Experience During the Lebanese War (1975-1976)". *Al-Surah al-Filastiniyah [Palestinian Image]*, First issue, 1978, Beirut: Muassaset al-Sinima al-Filastiniyah, p.19.

CHAPTER 7

Interview with Abu Thareef conducted on August 15th, 2016

CHAPTER 8

Sela, Rona. *li-Mo'ayyinat il-Jumhour: Hikayat Suwwar Filastiniyah 'Mo'taqilah' fil Archiffat al-Askariyyah Israiliyah [For the Public]*. Ramallah: Al-Madar, Al-Markez Al- Filastin lil Dirasat Al- Israiliyah, 2018.

Al-Surah al-Filastiniyah [Palestinian Image], First issue, Beirut: Muassaset al-Sinima al-Filastiniyah, 1978.

INDEX[1]

---

[1] Note: Page numbers followed by 'n' refer to notes.

Milton Keynes UK
Ingram Content Group UK Ltd.
UKHW020950250224
437982UK00007B/17